# HISTORIC STREETS
# OF LIVERPOOL

## DAVID PAUL

AMBERLEY

First published 2018

Amberley Publishing, The Hill, Stroud
Gloucestershire GL5 4EP

www.amberley-books.com

British Library Cataloguing in Publication Data.
A catalogue record for this book is available from the British Library.

ISBN 978 1 4456 7195 6 (print)
ISBN 978 1 4456 7196 3 (ebook)

Origination by Amberley Publishing.
Printed in Great Britain.

# CONTENTS

# INTRODUCTION

The streets of Liverpool that I have written about in this book in many respects reflect the constant element that permeates Liverpool's long – and sometimes illustrious – history: its river, the River Mersey. There still remains evidence that can be traced back to 1207, when King John granted letters patent to Liverpool – often referred to as a royal charter. To a large extent the king's action was prompted by the river and its strategic location, and it was the king himself who laid the blueprint for the town's original seven streets.

All of the streets explored are of particular merit or significance, whether it be with regards to the social, political or economic development of the city. However, regardless of social, political or economic considerations, the sheer beauty of the buildings is noteworthy in itself.

This very brief introduction to the streets of Liverpool aims to focus on some of the buildings that have moulded the development of the city. The book does not purport in any way to be an academic text, but is aimed at the general reader.

David Paul
Liverpool
June 2018

# 1. LIME STREET

The original Lime Street was laid out in 1790, at that time called Limekiln Lane by virtue of the fact that there were a number of lime works there – near to Lord Nelson Street and standing on the site upon which the famous Lime Street station was built. At that time the works, which were owned by William Harvey, were well outside of the town centre. In 1748, an infirmary was built by public subscription on the site that is now occupied by St George's Hall. The wings of the infirmary were specifically used as the Seamen's Hospitals, where old and dying seamen, together with their wives, could end their days. The upkeep and running costs of the Seamen's Hospitals were met by a levy of *6d* per month paid by every sailor leaving the port of Liverpool. After some years many of the physicians working at the infirmary objected to the smell, suggesting that the noxious fumes coming from the works were injurious to their patient's well-being. As a result, the kilns were removed from that location in 1804, but the street retained its name. Even up until 1812 there were few private residences in the area, as the land to the east of Skelhorne Street was the site of one of the town's major rope works.

Original Adelphi Hotel.

Adelphi Hotel.

Lime Street fields witnessed much brawling, especially on Sunday afternoons. The authorities eventually took action to stop such unsightly behaviour, but the area remained the town's centre of cockfighting and dogfighting, and was also noted as being the place where many local scores were settled. The cattle market was held in the area that is now occupied by the railway station, but in former times was held on open ground near to what is now South Castle Street. The market was established in many places over the years: first moving from South Castle Street to Chapel Street, then it went to St James's Place, then on to Church Lane before later moving to Lime Street, and finally in 1830 it moved to the Old Swan.

Our walk along Lime Street starts at the Adelphi end of the street. Strictly speaking, the Britannia Adelphi Hotel is not on Lime Street but rather Ranelagh Place, but that's a good enough place to start our walk along one of Liverpool's most famous streets.

## Ranelagh Gardens

Ranelagh Gardens, which opened in 1722, was Liverpool's first area for public recreation and was modelled on Ranelagh Gardens in Chelsea. When the gardens became less fashionable, two town houses were built on the site. The hotelier James Radley converted the houses into a hotel in 1826. Following the undoubted success of the original Adelphi Hotel, another was built on the same site some fifty years later. Then, with rail travel increasing, the Midland Railway bought the hotel in 1892, renaming it the Midland Adelphi Hotel. The current building was designed by Frank Atkinson and at the time of its opening was considered by many to be the 'most luxurious hotel outside London'. Over the years many famous guests have stayed at the Adelphi, including Franklin D. Roosevelt, Winston Churchill, Frank Sinatra, Judy Garland, Bob Dylan and Roy Rogers together with his horse, Trigger.

## The Vines

On the opposite corner is the Vines, known locally as the 'Big House'. The Vines was opened in 1867 by Albert B. Vines, but the establishment was bought in 1907 by Peter Walker, brewers of Warrington and Burton on Trent. In 1905, Walker also bought the Crown – located a little further along Lime Street.

The architect Walter Thomas was engaged to redesign the Vines; he'd also designed both the Philharmonic Dining Rooms and the Crown. Thomas was also credited with designing the Lewis's store building, which is just behind where we're standing. The male statue that proudly stands above the main entrance of what was the company's flagship

*Below left*: The Vines.

*Below right*: Dickie Lewis.

*Above*: Lime Street, *c.* 1940.

*Below*: Lime Street, *c.* 1907.

store is officially called *Liverpool Resurgent*, but is known locally as 'Nobby Lewis' or 'Dickie Lewis'. The statue, designed by Sir Jacob Epstein, was commissioned to mark the centenary celebrations of the store in 1956. Adverse trading conditions forced the company into liquidation in 2007; the final day of trading was 29 May 2010.

Walking along Lime Street from the Vines towards the Crown, it's obvious that there is significant redevelopment taking place. The current proposals for the Knowledge Quarter Gateway encompass the area around Brownlow Hill and Lime Street, including the Mount Pleasant car park and the ABC Cinema. The proposals for redevelopment in the area include student accommodation, a hotel and a number of retail outlets.

*Left*: St George's Hall.

*Below*: St George's Hall, *c.* 1906.

## Lime Street Station

Next we come to the iconic Lime Street station. When the Liverpool & Manchester Railway (L&MR) was first conceived the Liverpool terminal was at Crown Street, to the east of the city centre. The building work for the current station at Lime Street was not started until October 1833, after the cattle market on the site was bought from the council for £9,000. The council also agreed to pay £2,000 towards the cost of building Lime Street station, but gave a number of conditions. Once work had started a tunnel was dug from Edge Hill to Lime Street, and the station itself was finally opened by John Foster Jr in August 1836. Even at this time trains did not run directly into the station. Locomotives were decoupled at Edge Hill and the carriages used the force of gravity to carry them into the station. The carriages were then hauled out of the station on their return.

*Right*: Lime Street station, *c.* 1907.

*Below*: Lime Street station.

Rail travel became very popular with the public and by late 1842 – just six years after the station had opened – plans had to be drawn up to extend the station. A new station with an innovative iron segmental-arched-vault train shed was built by Sir William Tite and opened in 1849. However, further additions became necessary and in 1879 another train shed was added – the southern train shed. Following electrification of the lines, 1 January 1962 marked the beginning of the electric train services between Liverpool and Crewe. Later, in 1966, the InterCity services were started.

In 2007, the city celebrated its 800 anniversary and the following year held the designation of European Capital of Culture. In June 2009, statues of Ken Dodd (now Sir Ken) and Bessie Braddock – two of Liverpool's more famous citizens – were featured on the main concourse. As part of the celebrations, Lime Street station had a £35 million 'facelift', which was completed in 2010.

## North Western Hotel

With more and more people travelling to Liverpool, the London & North Western Railway built the North Western Hotel adjacent to Lime Street station. The hotel, built in 1879 to the design of Alfred Waterhouse, had a total of 330 guest rooms. But, as was the case with other high-end hotels in the city, the economic downturn of the 1920s precipitated the hotel's closure in 1933. For a relatively short while the building became known as Lime Street Chambers. After a long period when the building was unoccupied, John Moores University purchased the property and converted it into student accommodation. The hall of residence was opened in 1996.

North Western Hotel.

## St George's Hall

Directly across the road from the North Western Hall is the imposing St George's Hall, reputedly one of the finest examples of neo-Grecian buildings in the world, as acknowledged by the architectural historian Nikolaus Pevsner. Before St George's Hall was built the site was occupied by the first Liverpool Infirmary. As the city did not have any suitable venues for festivals and concerts, it was decided that money should be raised in order to build a suitable venue. The foundation stone for the hall was laid in 1838. Harvey Lonsdale Elmes, a young architect from London, won the competition to design the hall. Before building started in 1841 the plans were modified as it was decided that the hall needed to include law courts. The building opened in 1854 and was the first public building anywhere in the world to have air conditioning. In the early part of the twenty-first century the hall underwent major refurbishment, with Prince Charles reopening it on 23 April 2007.

St George's Plateau, lying between St George's Hall and Lime Street station, has statues of Prince Albert and Queen Victoria and a monument to Major-General William Earle. The centrepiece of the plateau, however, is the Grade I-listed Liverpool cenotaph, designed by L. B. Budden. The cenotaph is regarded as one of the finest war memorials in the country. In times of grief or triumph, people have traditionally gathered on the plateau.

## The Empire Theatre

The Empire Theatre stands at the corner of Lime Street and London Road, directly opposite to St George's Hall. On 15 October 1866 the New Prince of Wales Theatre and Opera House was the first theatre to be opened on the site. In 1867, its name was changed to the Royal Alexandra Theatre and Opera House. In 1894, the theatre closed, but was reopened under the ownership of Empire Theatre (Liverpool) Ltd. Then, in 1896, it was sold to Messrs Moss and renamed The Empire. The theatre closed in February 1924, and was demolished.

The design of the new theatre was based upon an American one. Unfortunately, in 'lifting' the design the architects failed to include provision for any bars, as no American theatres were permitted to serve alcohol at the time because of the laws of prohibition. This omission was quickly rectified! The theatre opened on 9 March 1925 and boasts the largest two-tier auditorium in Britain; it can seat 2,381 people. Many types of entertainment are hosted here including operas, variety shows, musicals, plays and pop concerts. The Beatles appeared here and there have also been two Royal Command Performances and a Royal Variety Performance.

The theatre remained open during the Second World War to entertain people during those difficult days, especially with the amount of bombing being focussed on Liverpool.

In 1979, Merseyside County Council acquired the theatre from Moss Empires and spent a considerable sum in improving backstage facilities. Further major improvements were made to it in 1999. In 2002, Clear Channel Entertainment became the owners, and the Ambassador Theatre Group took control of it in 2011.

*Above*: The original Empire Theatre.

*Below*: Empire Theatre.

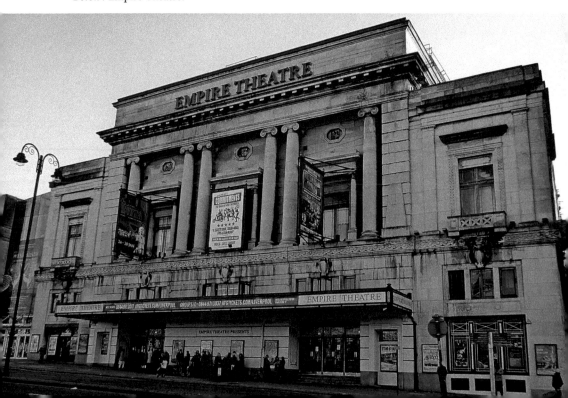

## Wellington's Column

Wellington's Column (or the Waterloo Memorial, as it is sometimes called) stands on the corner of William Brown Street and marks the end of Lime Street. The memorial is a monument to the Duke of Wellington and is a Grade II-listed building.

Many sites for Wellington's memorial were considered before the final site was adopted, including the top of Bold Street, Duke Street and Prince's Park. The foundation stone was laid by the lord mayor of Liverpool on 1 May 1861, but construction work was halted due to subsidence at the site. Although the memorial was inaugurated in 1863, it was not finally completed until 1865. The overall height of the memorial is 132 feet; the column, which stands on a plinth, is 81 feet high, and the statue itself is some 25 feet high. It is believed that the statue is fashioned from the melted-down bronze from cannons that were captured at the Battle of Waterloo. The statue faces south-east, ensuring that Wellington always faces the scene of his greatest victory: the Battle of Waterloo.

The pavement at the base of the column has an embedded brass strip that measures – exactly – the Board of Trade's 100 feet.

Wellington's Column.

# 2. WILLIAM BROWN STREET

The street that is now known as William Brown Street was originally called Shaw's Brow and was very different in character and aspect from the present one. Predominantly heathland, the area boasted a number of windmills – perhaps because of its high elevation.

At the beginning of the eighteenth century new industries were coming to Liverpool, together with a corresponding increase in the town's population. Shipbuilding and its concomitant industries were developing along the Mersey's shores, and other industries and trades were also finding a place in the flourishing town. A number of sugar refineries were located in Liverpool and the town was gaining a reputation for the beauty and accuracy of the timepieces that were now being manufactured. The area around Shaw's Brow, Islington and Dale Street was also developing a reputation as being the home of fine pottery manufacture.

James Shaw and his brothers were residents of Newton-in-the-Willows before coming to Liverpool. They came to the town as contractors for the building of St George's Church. In addition, they also made bricks from the excavations of the Old Dock and built in and around King Street. But the Shaws are principally noted for another industry that they introduced to the town in the early eighteenth century: the manufacture of earthenware.

General view of William Brown Street.

Their pot works was first established on the brow of the hill by Samuel Shaw. The pottery ovens were built on both sides of the road but most of the activity took place on the north side. Much of the production was subsequently moved to Dale Street, where Samuel's son, Thomas, owned a large mansion on the corner of Fontenoy Street. Other pot works soon became established on the Brow, and the industry grew to such an extent that the Brow had several different pot works and numerous workmen's cottages. Many of the proprietors of the works also chose to live on the Brow.

A famous potter who lived in Dale Street was Mr Chaffers. His pottery was on the north side of the Brow and he had moulding houses in Islington. His colourful and elegant pottery was manufactured from clay that was shipped directly from a mine in Cornwall. The Penningtons were another leading family in the area. Mr Pennington owned a pottery works on the Brow itself, while his eldest son, James, had a factory not far away at Copperas Hill. His second son, John, had his business near to Saint Anne Street, while Seth (Mr Pennington's youngest son) had his works on the Brow like his father. The businesses owned by the family became famous for manufacturing punch bowls and ornamental ware. There were other leading potters in the vicinity, including Mr Phillip Christian, whose works were located on the Brow, and Mr Zachariah Barnes, who had a pottery in the Old Hay Market. Indeed, when the census of 1790 took place it was recorded that there were seventy-four potters' houses inhabited by 374 people, all of whom were associated with the manufacture of pottery in some manner. Workers at the potteries were not known for their high wages and many who lived at the bottom of the Brow in the area known as St John's Tillage, were not averse to exhuming recently interred bodies in the hope that they could be sold to medical students working at the nearby infirmary, thus supplementing their meagre wages.

Looking down William Brown Street.

Shaw's Brow acquired its name as it was on the main coaching route out of Liverpool. This was an easterly direction via Dale Street and Townsend, but it was very steep, causing problems for coaches leaving the town. The route passed near to Mr Alderman Shaw's pottery on the Brow. Because of the abundance of the passing coach trade, the Brow was littered with a good many almshouses and the like.

In 1821, when Manchester Street was opened from Dale Street to St John's Lane, a different route out of town was established, even though the crest of the Brow had been lowered on several occasions. Shaw's Brow was widened in 1852.

Towards the end of the century, the potteries in Liverpool were facing increasing competition from potteries in the Midlands and, with the demise of Shaw's pot works and many of the other potteries, different industries soon sprung up in their wake. There was a coach factory, wheelwrights, grinding mills, a soap works and a number of builders' yards.

Before moving to the more recent history of William Brown Street, it's worth recounting a curious incident took place in the area early in 1830. A widow living with her daughter and son in Islington – a little further up from the Brow – required the services of a maidservant. As a result of the recommendation of a woman who owned a shop nearby in London Road, a young woman was interviewed and given the job. Although her appearance and dress left much to be desired, she was conscientious and diligent in her duties. In fact, on a number of occasions she displayed skills and expertise that would normally not be associated with someone from her class. She was a talented pianist and artist, and had extensive knowledge of medicine and the treatment of the sick. She also proved to be fluent in a number of foreign languages – not a common accomplishment for a person from the lower classes. Hannah Brade – her given name – also displayed exemplary fortitude during her period of employment. One day, when she was alone in the house, burglars entered and attempted to steal some valuables. Hannah soon saw them off! But, curiously, whenever guests arrived at the house, Hannah was always reticent to meet them for some reason.

Two years after joining the household, Hannah left her employment for no apparent reason, much to the dismay of the widow and her children. All contact and knowledge of her whereabouts was lost until a few months later, when a package was delivered to the home of her former employer. The parcel contained a number of lavish and expensive presents for members of the household, thanking them for the kindness that they had shown her during her period of employment. There was no forwarding address and there was no further contact with Hannah, so the mystery as to just who Hannah Brade was still remains.

## County Sessions House

William Brown Street, often referred to as the cultural quarter of the city, has so much to offer that it's worth taking some time to stroll down the street and maybe call into one or two of the many listed buildings in the area. Looking across from Wellington's Column – a good place to start walking along this short but historic street – we can see the County Sessions House, which stands just to the east of the Walker Art Gallery. Up until 1877 magistrates in Liverpool tried non-capital offences at the court in Basnett Street and at Kirkdale Sessions House, but changes in the legal system at this time meant that the courts had to find another venue. The new County Session House was designed in the late Victorian style by Liverpool architects Francis and George Holme, who had also designed the Homeopathic Hospital in Hope Street. Building work was started in 1882 and the first sitting in Islington took place on 4 August 1884.

The courthouse was one of the first in the country to be air-conditioned, but because of other economic considerations, the court had been designed with the main emphasis on visual appearance from the front. The rear of the building – similar to others along William Brown Street – is far more utilitarian in aspect, being built of brick.

Following the Courts Act of 1971, which curtailed all quarter sessions, the building was effectively redundant. It is now managed by the National Museums of Liverpool and houses a number of departments, including the Fine Art Curatorial and Learning Departments.

## Walker Art Gallery

A little further down, on the same side as the County Courthouse, we come to the Walker Art Gallery. The gallery itself was not established on its current site until 1877, but before that, following the Public Libraries Act of 1852, a library and museum opened in 1860. The new public library was the venue for the first Liverpool Autumn Exhibition, held in 1871. The success of this exhibition enabled the town's Library, Museum and Arts Committee to purchase in excess of 150 works of art over the next fifty years, perhaps one of the most famous being *And When Did You Last See Your Father?* by William Frederick Yeames.

In addition to enabling a public library and museum to be built, the Act of 1852 also made provision for an art gallery to be established in the town. In order to commemorate his term as mayor, local brewer Andrew Barclay Walker donated £20,000 towards the

Walker Art Gallery.

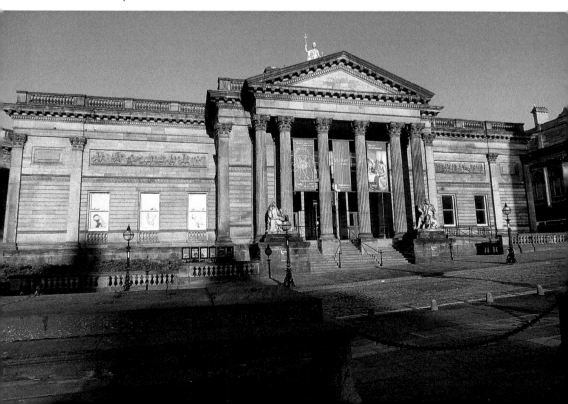

building of an art gallery in the town. The following year – 1874 – Prince Alfred, Duke of Edinburgh, laid the foundation stone. The gallery, named in honour of its founding benefactor, was designed by local architects Cornelius Sherlock and H. H. Vale, and opened on 6 September 1877 by Edward Henry Stanley, 15th Earl of Derby.

In 1893, the gallery was given long-term loan of the Liverpool Royal Institution's collection, and in 1948 the Institution gave the gallery the thirty-seven paintings from the William Roscoe collection it had acquired in 1819.

The Walker Art Gallery was the first public art gallery in the country and has been extended on two occasions – first in 1884, then again in 1933. The gallery's collection includes works by Degas, Rembrandt and Poussin, along with a major collection of Victorian and Pre-Raphaelite paintings. Works by twentieth-century artists such as David Hockney, Lucian Freud and Gilbert and George can also be seen in the gallery. *Cardinal Sin*, a statue by Banksy, was added to the gallery's collection in 2011. The Walker Art Gallery is part of the National Museums and Galleries on Merseyside.

## Steble Fountain

Walking down the street we come to Steble Fountain. It was in 1877 that a former mayor of the town, Lieutenant-Colonel Richard Fell Steble, offered £1,000 to the Improvement Committee of the town council so that a fountain could be erected on a plot of land at the top of William Brown Street – just to the west of Wellington's Column, between St George's Hall and the buildings on the far side of the street.

Michel Joseph Napoléon Liénard designed the fountain, which was unveiled in 1879 by the town's mayor. However, because the water pressure was very low, the resulting 'fountain' was little more than a trickle! The steam pump, which was located in the basement of Saint George's Hall, was replaced by a more efficient electric pump.

Steble Fountain in earlier times.

Steble Fountain.

Steble Fountain stands 23 feet high and is constructed from cast iron, with the circular base being 30 feet in diameter. An octagonal stem rises from the centre of the basin and a marine god stands at each corner of the cruciform base, representing Acis, Galatea, Neptune and Amphitrite. Above this there is a shallow octagonal bowl 8 feet in diameter, and at the top of the fountain there is a mermaid holding a cornucopia. Steble Fountain is a designated Grade II-listed building and was refurbished in 1992.

## Liverpool Central Library

On the far side of the road we come to what is often called the Picton Library, but is more correctly known as the Liverpool Central Library.

When St George's Hall was completed in 1854 it became necessary to demolish all of the properties along the Brow, which required an Act of Parliament. The alignment was also changed: the modified street now skirted the perimeter of St John's Churchyard. In its turn, this development freed a further area of land.

Prior to this, Mr J. A. Picton (later Sir James) brought a scheme before the town council that would establish a free public library in the town. His scheme was adopted. The first library was opened on 18 October 1852 and located in Dale Street; however, the library proved to be such a success that new and larger premises were soon being sought. William Brown (a local MP) donated land in order to build a public library and museum. Born at Ballymena, Brown was the eldest son of a Belfast linen merchant. After spending some time learning the trade at his father's business in America, Brown returned home in 1808. He then sailed to Liverpool, realising that the expanding port was the entry point for American exports. Then, after a number of years, he transferred his expertise in trading to merchant banking. Brown also became involved in politics and was elected to Parliament in 1846. He was re-elected on a further three occasions. When Brown had been made aware of the dire need for a public library in the town he financed the entire building costs, which amounted to £40,000.

Thomas Allom and the council's architect and surveyor Mr John Weightman designed the building, with William Brown himself laying the foundation stone on 15 April 1856. Brown's generosity not only provided funds for the new library, but also enabled a museum to be built on Shaw's Brow. The library, known as the William Brown Library and Museum, was opened on 18 October 1860. Somewhat modestly, Brown described it as a 'gift to the inhabitants of Liverpool'. Shortly after the opening of the library, the council voted to change the name of Shaw's Brow to William Brown Street.

Over the years, in order to accommodate the increasing collections, a number of extensions have been made to the library, the first being the opening of the Picton Reading Room in 1879, followed by the Hornby Library.

The foundation stone for the new circular reading room was laid in 1875 by the chairman of the William Brown Library and Museum, Sir James Allanson Picton, and it was later named the Picton Reading Room in his honour. The reading room was designed by Cornelius Sherlock and was the first electrical-lit library in the country. The Picton Reading Room was modelled after the British Museum Reading Room.

*Left*: Picton Reading Room.

*Below*: Looking towards St George's Hall.

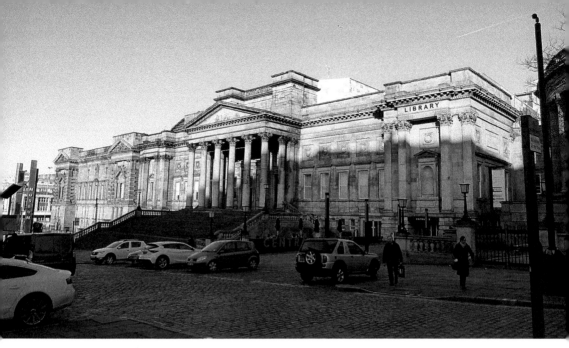

Central Library.

Standing directly behind the Picton Reading Room is the Hornby Reading Room, named in honour of Hugh Frederick Hornby, who bequeathed money for its construction to house his collection. The architect Thomas Shelmerdine designed the building and it opened in 1906. The Picton and Hornby Reading Rooms are two Grade II-listed buildings.

More recently it was recognised that, with changing technology, a radical new approach was needed in Liverpool's libraries. Following lengthy consultations and negotiations, it was decided to close the main library while extensive refurbishments were carried out to modernise it. The library closed its doors to the public on 23 July 2010 and reopened on Friday 17 May 2013.

## World Museum, Liverpool

Directly below the library complex is Liverpool's World Museum, but the first museum in the town was known as the Derby Museum. Towards the end of the nineteenth century there was no longer enough space for all of the artefacts housed in the William Brown Library and Museum, so a competition was held to design a suitable extension. The College of Technology and Museum extension opened in 1901. The number of exhibits continued to increase during the latter half of the twentieth century and early in the twenty-first century, the museum acquired more exhibition space in the former College of Technology. Because of the increasing diversity of the exhibits, the museum took the name of World Museum, Liverpool.

The museum's planetarium opened in 1970, which covers space exploration and the solar system. The museum's Egyptology collection (which includes objects from Egypt and Sudan) ranges from the Prehistoric to the Islamic period.

A number of new galleries have recently been opened in the museum, including World Cultures, the Bug House and the Weston Discovery Centre.

*Above*: World Museum, Liverpool.

*Left*: Former College of Technology.

## St John's Gardens

On the opposite side to the World Museum is St John's Gardens. In earlier times, because of the upwards slope of the land towards the east, the area of heath land known as the Great Heath was redolent with a large number of windmills and was an area much favoured for the public drying of washing. The area was first built upon when a general infirmary was opened in 1749. Later, the Seamen's Hospital was built in 1752, followed by a dispensary in 1778 and an asylum in 1789 – all in close proximity to one another. The area also attracted industrial enterprises such as limekilns, potteries, a rope works and a marble yard.

In 1767, the town's cemetery was located on the side of Shaw's Brow. The Church of St John the Baptist was built in the centre of the graveyard and dedicated in 1784. Documents in the Liverpool Records Office show that burials ceased on 11 June 1865 after

*Above*: Laying track in
William Brown Street, 1905.

*Right*: William Brown Street
from Old Haymarket.

82,491 people (including many French prisoners captured during the Napoleonic Wars) had been interred in the burial ground. Because of the building of St George's Hall, all of the other buildings in the area had to be demolished and the work of local industries relocated. Because of its close proximity to the hall, the church was demolished in 1898.

In 1888, a facility had been granted for the creation of a public garden in the area formerly occupied by the graveyard. The bodies were removed and interred elsewhere. Saint John's Gardens were designed by the city's surveyor, Thomas Shelmerdine, and opened in 1904 with the rather grand appellation of 'St John's Ornamental and Memorial Gardens'. There are seven memorial statues in the gardens, commemorating some of Liverpool's most notable citizens, including William Rathbone and William Ewart Gladstone.

## Queensway Tunnel

As our walk along William Brown Street draws to a close, we can look over towards the entrance to the original Birkenhead Tunnel, more correctly known as the Queensway Tunnel. The entrance to the tunnel is at Old Haymarket. A road tunnel going under the river had been proposed as early as 1825, but safety concerns were raised so the proposals were rejected. As motorised road traffic increased at the beginning of the twentieth century, long queues at the Mersey ferry terminal became an everyday occurrence. The Mersey Tunnel Act of 1925 enabled construction of the tunnel to proceed.

Sir Basil Mott was the tunnel's designer and during construction he worked in close partnership with John Brodie, the city engineer.

Much of the 1.2 million tons of clay that was excavated during construction was used as backfill for Otterspool Promenade – some way down the Mersey at Aigburth.

The tunnel took nine years to complete and was opened on 18 July 1934 by George V, watched by a crowd estimated at 200,000 people. When the tunnel was opened it was the longest road tunnel in the world, which had been built at a cost of £8 million. But, as early as 1960, the volume of traffic flowing through the tunnel had reached such a level that it was obvious another tunnel was needed in order to relieve congestion. The Kingsway Tunnel was opened in 1971.

Opening of Queensway Tunnel, 1934.

## Hillsborough Monument Memorial

The Hillsborough Monument Memorial is the final stop on our walk today; it stands at the bottom of William Brown Street in Old Haymarket. It commemorates the lives of the ninety-six Liverpool football supporters who lost their lives on 15 April 1989 while attending a football match between Liverpool FC and Nottingham Forest. The work – by sculptor Tom Murphy – was commissioned by the Hillsborough Justice Campaign. The circular monument has a particular design concept, which is meant to guides one's thoughts back to recall all that happened on that tragic day and the struggles that have been endured and overcome by the Hillsborough families since that time. The design depicts a number of figures representing Justice, Hope and Loss. The ninety-six people who lost their lives are represented as free-flying birds, all of whom are listed on the memorial.

*Right*: Hillsborough Disaster Memorial.

*Below*: Queensway Tunnel entrance.

# 3. DALE STREET

Looking towards the east, where the entrance to the Queensway Tunnel is located, there was a shallow valley or dale – hence the name Dale Street. In earlier times it was known as Dele Street, which is derived from the Saxon word for valley. The track then lead up towards the London road and, ultimately, on to Warrington and the road south to London.

It is believed that King John himself designed the original seven-street plan of Liverpool, which was in the form of a cross and included Dale Street. The first reference to Dale Street is in a deed from 1328. Plots of land were awarded to townsfolk by the king's bailiff. The strips of land usually comprised a dwelling at the front and an area for domestic cultivation towards the rear. Over the years, however, some of the plots began to be used for commercial purposes.

When you come to walk along Dale Street, the side streets also reveal much of Liverpool's hidden history. Starting from Manchester Street, just near the entrance to the original Queensway Tunnel, you pass Hatton Garden on the right. During the eighteenth century, Liverpool's population was growing at an alarming rate, mainly due to the prosperity being brought to the town by shipping and shipbuilding. This in turn meant that building developments were taking place right across the town, and the services of building workers were much in demand. It was at this time that two brothers, the Johnson brothers, moved to the town to set up their business. Having established their building yard, they named the access road that they had built Johnson Street, which still stands today. Fontenoy Street, North Street and Trueman Street were built at the same time. As the company prospered they bought some nearby gardens and fields, upon which they had plans to build a lime works. They constructed an access road and named it after their home village of Hatton near to Warrington. Because of the verdant location, the name Hatton Garden was soon adopted.

As the district developed, John Houghton, a local distiller whose premises were nearby, had an impressive property built at No. 139 Dale Street on the corner with Trueman Street. The house was later converted and became known as the Bull Inn. In 1797, Houghton had a church built in Hunter Street, Christ Church, which cost him somewhere in the region of £15,000.

Wyke's Court, near to Hatton Garden, was the home of John Wyke, a banker and watchmaker who brought watchmaking to Liverpool. Originally from Prescot, Wyke purchased the house immediately opposite the end of Crosshall Street, and in 1764/5 had the property completely rebuilt and called Wyke's Court. It was laid out for his residence, coach house, stables, garden, manufactory, warehouse and various other buildings all arranged about a large rectangular courtyard. The entrance to the property was on the south-west side under an archway from Dale Street. Here, John Wyke conducted his business as a watch- and clockmaker. The property later became the site of the Liverpool Gas Light Company.

As commerce developed in the town (due mainly to developing trade through the port) it was apparent the Dale Street was far too narrow for effective and efficient transport. The road was widened on several occasions and at great expense. Dale Street became the main street for land-based transport of goods and products both into and out of the town – the road to the turnpike being via Dale Street.

There were many packhorse and coaching inns dotted along the street, including The Angel and Crown, The Bull and Punch Bowl, and the Saracen's Head, all providing lodgings and board for travellers and also changes of horses for the coaches. The Golden Lion – also on Dale Street – was one of the oldest taverns in the town. When elections were called the inn became the headquarters of the Blue, or Gascoyne, Party. For many years the town was represented in Parliament by either General Isaac Gascoyne or his elder brother Bamber Gascoyne. In 1838, the tavern was replaced by a building erected by the Royal Bank. However, after the failure of the bank in 1867, the Queen Insurance Company bought the property for £95,000.

The Golden Fleece in Dale Street holds a unique place in Liverpool's history. It was from this inn, on 19 September 1760, that the first stagecoach to ever leave Liverpool departed the town. Previous to this there was no suitable road leading from the town that could accommodate wheeled carriages. Any goods or produce being conveyed between Liverpool and Manchester came via the Mersey and Irwell Navigation. Produce and goods from other inland towns was transported by packhorse, with groups of fifty to sixty packhorses leaving every day from the Golden Lion or the Fleece on their way to the north via the towns of Ormskirk and Preston. The packhorses returned carrying produce for local consumption or goods to be exported from the port. Later on, when the road was more passable, wagons drawn by eight horses were used instead. It was following the completion of the turnpike road to Prescot and Warrington in 1760 that this transformation could be accomplished. After that time coaches left the Golden Fleece on their two-day journey to London – in winter the journey could take three days or more. Passengers often went armed as there were sometimes encounters with highwaymen on the hazardous journey. As travel between towns became increasingly important, it became possible to take a coach from many of these inns to almost anywhere in the kingdom. At the eastern end of the street, which is where our walk starts from, there was a brook loosely following the present line of Byrom Street and Whitechapel.

When Dale Street was first widened it was thought that this would enable any amount of traffic to traverse the road, but this proved not to be the case. The road had to be widened again in 1819 and then again in 1828. During the widening many properties had to be demolished, but not all of the residents were willing to lose their homes or business premises. The authorities ran into particular problems, too, when they came to knock down properties near to Sir Thomas's Buildings. When all the buildings around were being demolished, a cobbler insisted on staying in his dwelling – much to the annoyance of the council authorities. Ultimately, he was compelled to leave. The same fate befell a barber who shared the same feelings as the cobbler. He too was unceremoniously removed from the premises as it was being demolished around him.

To further improve access to and from the town a new road was established at the eastern end of Dale Street, between Hatton Garden and St John's Lane. The new link road was called Manchester Street and offered an alternative for coaches leaving the town – rather than having to climb the steep Shaw's Brow.

Westminster Chambers.

## Westminster Chambers

Standing on the southern side of Dale Street, Westminster Chambers is located between Crosshall Street and Preston Street. The building, which has three storeys, an attic and a basement, has a number of modern shopfronts on the Dale Street side. The buildings originally had integral workshops and warehouses, and were designed by Richard Owens for David Roberts, Son & Co. The offices, which are predominantly housed at the front of the building, followed an elaborate stone Gothic design whereas the workshops are fashioned in plain brick. The building also has a number of carvings by Joseph Rogerson. The chambers were built in 1880, the year that Liverpool gained city status.

## Magistrates' Court

Looking directly across the road from Westminster Chambers is what was the Magistrates' Court. The court building was designed by John Grey Weightman and built between 1857 and 1859. It has a grand carriage entrance, designed so that magistrates could enter the court in a truly dignified manner. The main bridewell, also designed by Weightman, was built shortly afterwards in 1864. The court buildings and bridewell are Grade II-listed buildings. Weightman was trained as an architect in the offices of Charles Barry and Charles Robert Cockerell. Initially practicing alone in Sheffield, Weightman later became the Corporation surveyor in Liverpool, a role he held from 1848 to 1865. During his tenure

Former Magistrates' Courts.

he designed many of the town's most notable buildings, including the Magistrates' Courts, the Liverpool Free Library and Museum, and the Municipal Buildings (built between 1860 and 1866) – the Municipal Buildings were completed by Weightman's successor, Edward Robert Robson.

## Municipal Buildings

Towards the end of the nineteenth century there was considerable expansion in the city of Liverpool, necessitating a significant increase in the number of council employees. A new administrative building, the Municipal Buildings, was designed by the council's surveyor, John Weightman. The design of the building is considered to be a composite mixture of French and Italian Renaissance styles, with the iconic tower and its steeply pitched roof thought to be modelled on the central tower at Halifax Town Hall – designed by Charles Barry and his son, Edward Middleton Barry. Another feature worth noting is the sixteen sandstone figures around the balcony of the building representing the arts, sciences and industries of Liverpool. The clock tower in the centre of the building also has five bells hung in the so-called English style. Known simply as the New Public Offices when they were opened in 1867, the title was soon changed to the Municipal Buildings. Council meetings were held there from January 1868.

*Above and left*: The Municipal Buildings.

Because of a number of factors – particularly the high operating and maintenance costs – it was decided that the building was 'surplus to requirements' in 2016. It now looks as though the Singapore-based property company Fragrance Group Ltd (FGL) has won the bidding battle and will acquire the property on a 250-year lease. The council currently has in excess of 600 members of staff who work in the offices, but they will be relocated to office accommodation in the Cunard Building and other council offices.

## Municipal Annex

The building that is often locally referred to as the Municipal Annex stands on the corner of Dale Street and Sir Thomas Street, and was originally built as the Conservative Club. The five-storey building was designed by the architects F. & G. Holme. The lavishly appointed building had a number of reception rooms where members could entertain their guests, and there were first-class dining facilities and also a billiard room – a favourite pastime.

With the increasing – but necessary – bureaucracy in the city, the building was converted into Municipal Offices between the world wars and used as council offices until it was sold in the 1990s. After some years of neglect, the building was completely refurbished and opened in 2015 as a DoubleTree hotel by Hilton.

Municipal Annex.

*Above*: Imperial Chambers.

*Left*: Dale Street, 1907.

Muskers Buildings.

## Muskers Buildings

A little further along from the Municipal Annex and Imperial Chambers we arrive at the Muskers Buildings, originally opened as the Junior Reform Club. Built in the early 1880s in the Gothic Revival style to the design of Thomas E. Murray, the red-sandstone building has a number of canted bays with two-storey oriel windows. Since then the building has undergone extensive refurbishment and has been converted to luxury office accommodation.

## Prudential Assurance Building

Next we come to the Prudential Assurance Building, constructed between 1885 and 1886 to the designs of Alfred Waterhouse. Built predominantly from red-pressed brick and terracotta, it certainly makes an unmistakable statement along the Dale Street skyline. Waterhouse's son Paul (also an architect) was commissioned to add a tower to the building in 1905.

The Prudential Assurance Building has gained a certain notoriety, but not for any reason connected with its architecture. The story concerns one of its insurance salesmen, a certain William Herbert Wallace. Wallace, a very intelligent man, had worked for the Prudential for fifteen years and lived with his wife Julia (seventeen years his senior) in the Anfield area of the city. On the evening of Tuesday 20 January 1931, Wallace was asked to interview a prospective client living in Mossley Hill. When he arrived at the district he searched the area, but found that there was no such address. On returning home, Wallace could not gain entry. After repeated attempts he was finally able to enter the house, only to find that his wife had been brutally murdered. Following a police investigation littered with errors and inconsistencies, Wallace was charged with the murder and went for trial at Liverpool Assizes. He was found guilty and sentenced to death by hanging; however, the sentence was quashed by the Court of Criminal Appeal on the grounds that it was 'not supported by the weight of the evidence'. Wallace continued to work for the Prudential Assurance Company, albeit in a different capacity, but just two years after his acquittal he died of natural causes.

For a time the building was owned by Redefine International, but was sold to an undisclosed buyer in 2014.

*Above*: Shops along Dale Street, 1890.

*Left*: Prudential Assurance Building.

## The Temple

Adjacent to the Royal Insurance Building is the Temple, which was built between 1864 and 1865. The Temple was commissioned by the banker Sir William Brown and designed in an Italianate style by Sir James Picton. The entrance to the building is particularly noteworthy, showing a carving of four clasped hands together with the inscription 'Harmony Becomes Brothers'.

*Above left*: The Temple.

*Above right*: Royal Insurance Building.

## Royal Insurance Building

Built towards the end of the nineteenth century, the Royal Insurance Building stands on the corner of Dale Street and North John Street. The Liverpool-based architect James Francis Doyle designed the Grade II-listed building. Doyle had been selected through an open competition to design the building and the final decision was made by Norman Shaw, who was familiar with Doyle's work having collaborated with him on the design of the White Star Building in the city.

The structure – unique at the time – incorporates a steel framework supporting the Edwardian baroque façade of granite and Portland stone. Following major renovation and refurbishment, the building has now been transformed into the upmarket Aloft Hotel.

## Rigby's Building

Across the road stands the impressive Rigby's Building. Rigby's takes its name from Alderman Thomas Rigby, who bought the building in 1852 in order to further his business enterprises – mainly hotels and public houses. At that time the property was known as the Atherton Buildings. It is thought that the present building dates from around 1850, but there is evidence to suggest that the original property was built as far back as 1726. Rigby's Buildings is designated as a Grade II-listed building.

Rigby's Building.

## Union Marine Buildings

Union Marine Buildings (on the corner of Hackins Hay) was designed by Sir James Picton and was originally erected in 1859 for the Queen Insurance Company.

The Union Marine & General Insurance Co. Ltd first received its Certificate of Incorporation in January 1863 and shortly after, on 2 February 1863, opened for business in Liverpool. The company was created following a merger between Charles Langton & Co. and Rawson, Aikin & Co. Ltd. The company acquired the International Marine Insurance Co. Ltd in 1893 and then later merged with the Phoenix Co. in 1911. In 1905, the company moved into the Union Marine Buildings and changed its name to the Union Marine & General Insurance Co. Ltd in 1931.

## State Insurance Building

Towards the end of our walk is the State Insurance Building – at No. 14 Dale Street. The architect of the State Insurance Building, Walter Aubrey Thomas, was also the designer of the Royal Liver Building and Tower Buildings. Since opening in 1906, the building has served a number of purposes: at one time being a dance hall and then later, after being temporarily closed following a bombing raid during the Second World War, it was reopened as a branch of Debenhams. At the end of the twentieth century the property was used as a nightclub.

Liverpool,
London and Globe
Building.

## Liverpool, London and Globe Building

At the very end of our walk along Dale Street and standing next to the Town Hall is the Liverpool, London and Globe Building. It was designed by Charles Robert Cockerell, the architect of St George's Hall and the nearby Bank of England Building. Christopher F. Heyward and Frederick Pepys Cockerell (Charles's son) also contributed to the design. Constructed between 1856 and 1858, the Liverpool, London and Globe Building is Grade II listed.

## Note

It is alleged that between 1912 and 1913 Adolf Hitler lived in Liverpool while he avoided conscription in his native Austria. While the veracity of this claim is open to question, it is a matter of fact that at that time his half-brother Alois Hitler Jr and his wife, Bridget Hitler, managed a restaurant in Dale Street.

# 4. CASTLE STREET

Castle Street is one of the original seven streets of Liverpool, mapped out when King John gave the town its charter in 1207. Our walk along this historic street starts at the town hall, visits Exchange Flags, the Nelson Monument, and continues as far as the Victoria Monument in Derby Square.

Having been granted its charter, Liverpool soon adopted the king's official seal, which incorporated the eagle of St John holding a twig of broom in its beak. The seal remained the official seal of Liverpool until it was lost in 1644. When the new seal was adopted the eagle had been replaced by a cormorant and the sprig of broom by laver (seaweed). Over the years the cormorant has been transformed into the mythical liver bird.

Castle Street was acknowledged to be the centre of the old town, running between the high cross and the castle. Sir James Allanson Picton (the first chairman of Liverpool's Library and Museum Committee) said that 'the history of Castle Street is the history of Liverpool', and that sentiment can be readily understood when considering the plethora of historic buildings in the short length of the street. Many of the former bank buildings along Castle Street were originally built to cope with the huge wealth coming into the town as a direct result of the slave trade.

There was a market held every Saturday, covering an area at the northern end of Castle Street, High Street and part of Dale Street, with different commodities being sold in different areas. There was also segregation of the traders: spaces on the eastern side of the street were reserved for merchants from Lancashire, whereas merchants coming from Cheshire were allocated spaces on the western side of the street. Before the start of trading, the mayor, together with his 'levelookers', inspected the produce to ensure that the correct measures were being offered for sale. For the first hour after the opening of the market, only freemen of the town were allowed to purchase goods.

There were also two charter fairs held in the town, each lasting for approximately twenty days. The earlier fair date was 25 July, though the fair itself started ten days before that date and ended ten days afterwards. Similarly, the second fair was held on 11 November but also started ten days before and ended ten days after. During the times of the fairs debtors could walk freely without the fear of imminent arrest, providing they were pursuing their lawful business.

The Sanctuary Stone is the only remaining evidence to indicate the boundary of the market. The fairs, which were extensive, covered the area near to the present Exchange Flags and Exchange Buildings, and went right through to Castle Street. There was a great show of ceremony when the town's mayor and other officials, including the bailiffs, walked through the fair accompanied by a band of strolling players. The mayor held a banquet following the ceremonial walk. Over the years the fairs began to dwindle in their importance and eventually ceased through lack of interest.

Robert Williamson owned a printing house on Castle Street near to Brunswick Street, where he produced Liverpool's very first newspaper, *The Williamson's Advertiser*, the first edition of which appeared on 25 May 1756. This was followed nine years later, on 27 December 1765, by *The Gore's Advertiser*. It's owner, John Gore, also had a printing and stationary establishment on Castle Street, from which he printed the first Liverpool Directory in 1766. Mr Thomas Bean's *Albion* newspaper had its offices at the corner of Brunswick Street. A bookseller on Castle Street called Mr Hodgson started the *Liverpool and Lancaster Weekly Herald* in 1788.

Castle Street only ran as far as the current Harrington Street as the trench around the castle barred any further passage. Originally, the street was only 5 yards wide for most of its length, but widened out towards the Town Hall end. In 1786, an Act of Parliament allowed for the much-needed widening of Castle Street, thus enabling many of the slum houses and tenements in close proximity to the Town Hall to be demolished. In addition to the widening of Castle Street, Water Street, Chapel Street and Fenwick Street were also widened, but owing to the expense that would have been incurred, not all of the street-widening plans were carried out.

## Town Hall

The Town Hall, which is where our walk starts, is situated at the junction of Castle Street, High Street, Water Street and Dale Street. It is a Grade I-listed building and is recognised as one of the best examples of eighteenth-century town halls, having one of the finest suites of civic rooms in the country.

Liverpool Town Hall.

In all probability, the first building in Liverpool to be used as a town hall dates back to 1515 and reputedly had a thatched roof. The building was replaced in 1673 by a more substantial building, said to stand on 'pillars and arches of hewen [sic] stone'. The Town Hall of 1673 also served as a meeting place for merchants and traders to conduct their commercial activities in the area under the elevated Town Hall. However, towards the middle of the eighteenth century, trade being transacted through the town and port of Liverpool had grown to such an extent that it was decided that a new, grander Town Hall needed to be built – both to reflect the increasing volume of trade and also to make a public statement as to the growing importance of the town.

The current Town Hall was built between 1749 and 1754 to a design by John Wood, often described as 'one of the outstanding architects of the day'. James Wyatt was commissioned to design an extension, which was added in 1785; however, just ten years after its completion there was a disastrous fire that necessitated almost the whole of the premises being rebuilt. Wyatt used the situation to add a massive central dome and sometime later, working in conjunction with the town's surveyor, John Foster, a two-storey Corinthian portico was added. The ground floor was, in effect, a trading floor for merchants to exchange their goods, having a courtyard in the centre surrounded and supported by a series of Doric colonnades; but, because of a number of shortcomings (mainly the darkness of the area) traders often carried out their business in the street directly behind.

The Town Hall has also been the focus of a number of acts of sabotage or treason. In 1775, during the American Revolution, trade between the two countries was badly disrupted, causing many shipowners to lay-off sailors or reduce their wages. This, in turn, caused an outcry and seamen's strike. At the time there were upwards of 3,000 sailors out of work in Liverpool. At one point unarmed sailors were fired upon and the resulting melee led to several deaths. An assault with cannon was made on the Town Hall, where some shipowners were taking shelter; in order to restore order the military was called from Manchester. Many years later – in 1881 – the Town Hall was once again under siege. This time from the Fenians, who aimed to blow it up, though their attempt was unsuccessful.

One of the very last acts of the American Civil War was enacted in Liverpool. In November 1865, in an action of total surrender, Captain Waddell (master of the CSS *Shenandoah*) made his way to the Town Hall and presented a letter to the mayor, effectively surrendering his vessel to the British government.

During the Second World War, due to constant and repeated Luftwaffe attacks on Liverpool, the Town Hall (and many other buildings in the city) sustained severe damage.

The Town Hall was given a face-lift between 2014 and 2015, as the outside of the building was in need of cleaning due to the effects of pollution.

The layout of the interior of the building is very simple in concept, with the ground floor being used as the council chamber. There is also a Hall of Remembrance at this level, which was completed in 1921 and has a number of panels that commemorate all of the men from Liverpool who lost their lives on active service during the First World War. Eight murals painted by Frank O Salisbury in 1923 complete the memorial.

One of the most impressive features of the interior of the Town Hall is the Staircase Hall, described in the Buildings of England series as 'one of the great architectural spaces of Liverpool'. The city's motto is inscribed around the base of the dome, directly above the staircase, '*Deus Nobis Haec Otia Fecit*'. The quotation is taken from the Roman poet Virgil and translates as 'God has given to us this leisure,' or, more loosely, 'God has bestowed these blessings on us'.

The balcony at the north side of the building is known as the Queen's Balcony. This relates to the occasion in 1851 when Queen Victoria stood there and greeted the town's merchants standing in Exchange Flags below. Apparently, the queen is then alleged to have commented that she had never before seen together such a large a number of well-dressed gentlemen.

The building now serves more as a civic suite rather than an administrative centre, with that function being discharged around other offices in the city. Conducted tours around the Town Hall enable members of the general public to view the civic rooms and council chambers.

## Exchange Flags

Moving to the northern side of the Town Hall, we come to the area known as Exchange Flags. It is the original trading site for the town's merchants, where they would meet to conduct their business in the open air. Business was interrupted when it rained and the area became waterlogged and muddy, often forcing merchants to continue their business indoors. The area was later flagged and from that time onwards business transactions became known as 'trading on the flags'.

The commercial heart of Liverpool has always been centred around the Town Hall. John Foster, the Corporation of Liverpool's senior surveyor, designed the first Exchange Building in a neoclassical style – he was possibly working with James Wyatt. The Exchange was built between 1803 and 1808.

A building designed by Thomas Henry Wyatt in the Flemish Renaissance style was constructed between 1864 and 1867. The business of trading in the open continued until later in the century, but as the new Cotton Exchange featured the latest technology of the day and had direct links to the world's major cotton markets (including New York, Bombay and Bremen), traders were forced indoors to conduct their business.

Exchange Flags, *c.* 1851.

The buildings that currently enclose Exchange Flags are Walker House (formerly known as Derby House) on the western side of the flags and Horton House – named after Admiral Sir Max Horton – on the east. The building complex was designed by Gunton & Gunton. Significant modifications were made during construction so that the buildings could be adapted to operate as the Western Approaches Command headquarters during the Second World War. It was from this command centre that Admiral Sir Max Horton planned and directed the campaign against the German submarine fleet – the Battle of the Atlantic being one of the most critical campaigns of the war.

## Nelson's Monument

Following the death of Admiral Horatio Nelson at the Battle of Trafalgar, the town council launched an appeal to raise sufficient funds to erect a suitable monument in his honour. The council gave £1,000 to the fund and in less than two months almost £9,000 had been raised from public donations. One of Liverpool's leading campaigners for the abolition of slavery, William Roscoe, initiated the fundraising campaign for the monument. The monument, which stands to the north of the Town Hall towards the centre of Exchange Flags, was designed by Matthew Cotes Wyatt and sculpted by Richard Westmacott. Erection of the monument started in July 1812 and it was unveiled on 21 October 1813, the eighth anniversary of Nelson's death. There is an inscription at the top of the pedestal, which reads 'ENGLAND EXPECTS EVERY MAN TO DO HIS DUTY'. A figure representing Death stands to Nelson's right and is seen reaching out to touch him. Britannia is standing behind Nelson holding a laurel wreath together with his decorations. Nelson's Monument was the first public sculpture to be erected in Liverpool and is Grade II listed.

Nelson Monument.

Midland Bank Building.

## Midland Bank Building

Leaving Exchange Flags and returning to Castle Street, the first building on the eastern side of the street is still known as the Midland Bank Building. It has Grade II-listed status and was originally built for the art dealers Thomas Agnew & Co. The three-storey brick building is in the Queen Anne style and was designed by the architects Salomons, Wornum & Ely. A distinctive feature of the building is the deep frieze at the top with swags and wreaths.

It was during the 1960s that Raymond Fletcher of Bradshaw, Rowse & Harker designed what was to become the Castle Street office of the Midland Bank, the branch having been transferred from No. 62 Castle Street. When Midland Bank was acquired by HSBC Holdings plc in 1992 the bank was branded under the HSBC banner until it closed in 2009. Since that time the building has served as a mini-supermarket.

## British and Foreign Marine Insurance Company Building

Many of the buildings that adorn Castle Street were built during the Victorian era, when Liverpool's commerce and maritime enterprises were pre-eminent. To a large extent this is reflected in the grandeur of the buildings, especially in the area near to the Town Hall in the Dale Street, Castle Street and Water Street district.

Immediately adjacent to the Midland Bank Building is the British and Foreign Marine Insurance Company Building, which was built for the company between 1888 and 1890. Much of the design is said to be the work of G. E. Grayson, a partner in the locally based architectural firm of Grayson & Ould. The mosaics on the outside of the building were designed by Frank Murray but were made by the Italian glass and mosaic manufacturers Salviati. The red sandstone offices are typical of others built at the time for insurance companies, banks and the like, many of whom had their head offices based in Liverpool because of the burgeoning maritime trade. The adjoining building, the Queen Insurance Building, was also designed by Grayson & Ould.

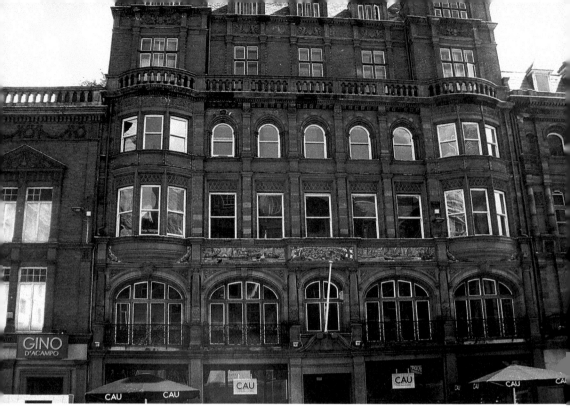

British and Foreign Marine Insurance Co. Building.

The building is particularly symmetrical in its design, having five storeys and attics in five bays. Fittingly for a marine insurance building, the property incorporated a mosaic frieze depicting shipping scenes immediately above the first floor. Another striking feature of the design is the two-storey oriel windows.

The company was established in the 1860s and only ceased trading in 1967. The building in Castle Street was the company's headquarters for almost seventy years.

## Midshires Building Society

The building directly across the road at Nos 2–4 Castle Street dates from 1882 and was originally built for the jewellers Robert Jones & Sons. At one point the building served as a branch of the Midshires Building Society and later on it was used as yet another branch of the National Westminster Bank. Like so many other buildings in the street the architect chose to follow the French Renaissance style, with bands of polychromatic stone, granite facing and a red-tiled roof. The building is now owned by Starbucks.

## Cheltenham & Gloucester Building Society and NatWest Branches

The building occupying Nos 6–8 Castle Street was built in 1897 and bears the name of the Cheltenham & Gloucester Building Society; however, most of the other buildings as far as Brunswick Street are, or have been, branches of the National Westminster Bank.

*Above left*: National & Provincial Building Society Building.

*Above right*: National Westminster Branch.

Standing on the western side of the street, the National Westminster Bank Building was designed by Norman Shaw for the former Parr's Bank. Similar in outward appearance to the White Star Building on the corner of James Street and the Strand (also designed by Shaw – in conjunction with James Francis Doyle), the building is not as striking but continues with Shaw's signature striped effect. He also retains the large round-headed and rusticated entrance to the building. The building was constructed between 1899 and 1902.

National Westminster
Overseas Branch.

Although known as the National Westminster Bank Overseas Branch, the next building on the corner of Castle Street and Brunswick Street is very different from its neighbour, having been designed by Grayson & Ould – the architects who designed the British & Foreign Marine Insurance Company at Nos 3–5 Castle Street. The design is a variant of the French Renaissance style.

## Bank of England and Norwich Union Buildings

On the eastern side of the street on the corner of Castle Street and Cook Street stands the former Bank of England Building, which was designed by Charles Robert Cockerell and built between 1845 and 1848. The Victorian neoclassical design is considered to be Cockerell's finest work. Somewhat deceptive in its appearance, by incorporating a portico of four attached Doric pillars Cockerell conveys the impression of the building being significantly larger than it actually is. Before the Bank of England Building was built, the site was occupied by the Liverpool Arms Inn.

More recently, the Grade I-listed building attracted a degree of media attention due to a standoff with police when it was being illegally occupied by the Love Activists, who were using the vacant building as a shelter for the homeless of Liverpool.

The Norwich Union Building, which stands next to its more illustrious neighbour, was at one time a branch of the Huddersfield Building Society and is now the Castle Street Townhouse.

*Below left*: Norwich Union Building.

*Below right*: Bank of England Building.

## Former Co-operative Bank

The building that stands on the southern side of the corner of Castle Street and Brunswick Street was once the Liverpool headquarters of the Co-operative Bank. However, the building, which was designed by the flamboyant architect William Douglas Caröe and built between 1890 and 1892, was originally the headquarters of the Adelphi Bank. The building has a particularly distinctive appearance, with bands of sandstone and granite contrasting with the corner turret that is surmounted by the green copper onion dome. Special note should be taken of the magnificent bronze doors, featuring reliefs by the London sculptor Thomas Stirling Lee. The doors show scenes of male friendship, depicting Achilles and Patroclus, Roland and Oliver, David and Jonathan, and Castor and Pollux.

Co-operative Bank Building.

## No. 62 Castle Street

No. 62 Castle Street was designed by Liverpool architects Lucy & Littler and built on the western side of the street in 1868. Two of the main architectural features of the building were the domed banking hall and the Corinthian columns. Two bays designed by George Enoch Grayson (another architect based in Liverpool) were later added to the building. When the foundations for the bank were being dug, relics from the castle moat were uncovered. Originally built for the Alliance Bank, at the time of opening a Mrs Child advertised Child's New Chop House and Restaurant, which offered wines and smoking rooms and was located under the bank itself. It was described as being the 'coolest room in town'.

Shortly after opening, the bank was faced with financial problems, and in 1871 the branch was sold to the National Bank. In 1873, the North & South Wales Bank moved its headquarters into the premises as they had outgrown their existing premises in James Street. At its zenith there was over 300 staff based in the branch, but by the beginning of the twentieth century the bank's business began to decline, which resulted in amalgamation with the Midland Bank in November 1908. The premises remained as a Midland branch until the early 1980s when the business was transferred to the other end of the street – at the corner of Dale Street opposite to the Town Hall. The building was then totally refurbished in 1990 and reopened as an upmarket twenty-bed, all-suite hotel known as Trials Hotel. In 2004, the hotel was bought by Centre Island Hotels, remodelled, refurbished and reopened as No. 62 Castle Street.

*Below left*: Looking along Castle Street.

*Below right*: No. 62 Castle Street.

Victoria Monument

Our walk along Castle Street comes to an end as we approach the Victoria Monument at the southern end of the street. The monument, a Grade II-listed structure that was unveiled on 27 September 1906, is built on the site of Liverpool Castle. It was designed by E. M. Simpson, Professor of Architecture at Liverpool University, working in conjunction with the architectural firm of Willink & Thicknesse. The four groupings of twenty-six bronze figures around the memorial represent Agriculture, Commerce, Education and Industry, and are the work of Charles John Allen, vice principal of the School of Art and an exponent of the New Sculpture movement. Other works by Allen can be seen in the city: he has two allegorical panels at St George's Hall and a frieze at the Royal Insurance Building in Dale Street depicting themes relating to insurance, but it is his work on the Victoria Monument that is considered to be his masterpiece.

Victoria Monument.

# 5. WATER STREET

Like the adjacent Castle Street, Water Street is one of the seven original streets as laid down by King John himself. For many years the street was known as Bonke Street – so named because in the Lancashire dialect of the time 'bonke' was the word for the bank of a river, and Bonke Street led down from the town to the water's edge. The name changed to Bank Street and then gained its current appellation of Water Street in the early sixteenth century.

After crossing the Mersey, travellers from Chester and beyond were deposited at the bottom end of the street. The monks of Birkenhead, or Byrkheved as it was often written, had the sole concession to operate the ferry and were allowed to charge a modest fee for transporting people and goods across the river – 2*d* for a mounted rider or 1*d* for a man and his wares on market day. The monks also owned a property in the street: Jonathan Hunter's Hoose. It served two purposes, firstly it was used as a resting place for travellers when bad weather prevented crossings taking place, and secondly it was used to store any grain that the monks had failed to sell.

A mark of the Water Street's importance and eminence is evident as it was equipped with its own sewerage system as early as 1831, a time when most other streets in the town still had open sewers.

Being a sea port, there were a number of hostelries along the street. One of the more famous was the King's Arms Inn, whose landlord at one time was Daniel Dale. Dale used to allow his head waiter, known as 'Black Matthew', to sit in the cellar on the afternoon of George IIIs birthday and invite well-wishers to come and drink a toast to the king – the drink normally being the landlord's best port. This ritual would continue until 'Black Matthew' fell off his stool!

## Barclays Bank Building

The Barclays Bank Building is situated on the north side of Water Street and was opened on 24 October 1932. Their banking history, however, goes back to 1773 when Benjamin and Arthur Heywood founded Heywood's Bank. The brothers had acquired their wealth through profits from the slave trade, having been engaged in at least 125 slaving voyages. The bank was then incorporated into the Bank of Liverpool, whose headquarters at the top of Water Street had replaced the famous Talbot Inn coaching house in 1832. Martins Bank and the Bank of Liverpool merged in 1918 to form the Bank of Liverpool and Martin's Ltd. The name was changed to Martins Bank Ltd (without an apostrophe) in 1928. Martins Bank was bought by Barclays Bank in 1969. At that time, all of its 700 branches became branches of Barclays.

*Above left*: Barclay's Bank Buildings, 1948.

*Above right*: Barclay's Bank Buildings.

When it was decided that a new headquarters needed to be built, three architects from Liverpool and three architects from London were approached and asked to submit suitable designs for the building. Herbert J. Rowse's classical Roman revivalist design was chosen. Noted for its unique construction, the building has nine floors above ground level together with a mezzanine floor and three floors below ground. The building's foundations extend 50 feet under the building. Constructed on a steel frame, the building has reinforced-concrete floors and stairs, making it virtually fireproof. On the outside, the external walls are of brick faced with Portland stone, which actually increases in whiteness following lengthy periods of exposure to the atmosphere.

The building is acknowledged as being Rowse's masterpiece, ranking among the very best interwar classical buildings in the country. To say that the banking hall is opulent would be a gross understatement as it ranks among the most sumptuous banking halls ever envisaged.

Much of the first floor was reserved for the bank's administration staff. The bank's chairman, general manager, his assistant and secretaries all had their offices along the Water Street side of the building. The conference room was also located there. Most of the other floors were rented out as tenantable office accommodation. The boardroom suite, dining rooms and kitchen were all located on the eighth floor. At the top of the building – the ninth floor – there was an apartment designed for use by the chairman. The roof area also boasted a garden that was enclosed by colonnades.

When awarded Grade II-listed status it was cited that the building was essentially a Liverpool building, but that it also embodied American classicism as promoted through Charles Reilly's Liverpool School of Architecture

During the Second World War much of the Bank of England's gold was stored in the bank's vaults, directly below the banking hall. Operation Fish was the code name of the operation that transported 280 tons of the nation's gold reserves during May 1940 from London to Martins Bank head office in Water Street, before being shipped to safety in Canada.

Castlewood Property has owned the building at No. 4 Water Street since 1996. In June 2014, Liverpool City Council gave approval for changing the use of the building to a 138-bedroom five-star hotel, but as yet development has not commenced.


## India Building

A little lower down on the southern side of the street is the India Building. The original India Building was built by George Holt (Alfred Holt's father), who had the idea of building a block of offices so that shipowners could conduct their business in conducive surroundings rather than in dark and dreary counting houses. It is rumoured that Holt took the precaution of making the outer walls particularly strong so that the building could easily be converted into warehouses in the event of his idea failing to materialise. The foundation stone was laid in 1833.

When it was decided that the original building had outgrown its usefulness, a number of architects were asked to submit designs for a new building. The competitive process, assessed by Giles Gilbert Scott, awarded the design contract to Arnold Thornely and Herbert James Rowse – the architect who had designed the Barclays Bank Building. Richard Durning Holt and Alfred Holt & Co., known as the Blue Funnel Line, built the property as a speculative venture, the intention being to use part of the building for their company's offices and then to let the remaining offices to other businesses.

Because of the complexity of the new building it had to be constructed in two stages. Part of the building was constructed alongside the existing one before it could be demolished. As the new building straddled the former Chorley Street, Liverpool Corporation had stipulated that an arcade of shops must be established through the centre of the building – in effect replacing the former street. As had been the original intention, Alfred Holt & Co. occupied three of the floors and the other floors were let to other commercial enterprises.

Built between 1924 and 1932 in the Italian Renaissance style, the building has nine storeys, a mezzanine, a basement and a sub-basement and is constructed on a steel frame and clad in Portland stone – a style and technique used in a number of other building designed by Rowse. The characteristic work of Edward C. Thompson can be seen all around the building. Rowse commissioned the sculptor to work on many of his buildings in the city. The carved figure of Neptune kneeling in a scallop shell and two reclining tritons reflect maritime connections of the building.

When India Buildings was raised to Grade II* status on 5 November 2013, one of the main reasons cited for the elevation was its transatlantic influence, which reflected the city's historic links with the United States. The citation actually stated that it 'emulates the most impressive early twentieth-century commercial buildings of the US'.

There is, however, a darker side to the building's history. The property was used as collateral to secure large loans; loans that were in excess of the value of the buildings.

*Above left*: India Buildings.

*Above right*: Water Street, 1892.

The company obtaining the loans was operated by Achilleas Kallakis and Alexander Williams, who were jailed for fraud in January 2013.

India Buildings was badly damaged during the Blitz of May 1941. After the war it was restored to its original condition, with the work being completed in 1953.

An Irish company, Green Property, bought India Buildings in 2009.

## Oriel Chambers

Looking across to the other side of the street we can see the unique Oriel Chambers. Peter Ellis, a Liverpool architect, was commissioned to design it by Revd Thomas Anderson. The building is Grade I listed and the first building in the world to feature a metal-framed glass curtain wall. The revolutionary design features a matrix of oriel windows with each panel encased in an iron frame, thus enabling the maximum amount of light to enter the building, and, at the same time, define it. There was one other principle that Ellis adopted in the building's design and that was the extensive use of precast, reinforced-concrete columns, which gave integral strength to the building. Having an area of some 43,000 square feet, the five-storey building is a classic example of modernist architecture; however, by all accounts when it opened in 1864 the building's design was not universally acclaimed as being of any particular merit. Indeed, it received much adverse criticism.

Oriel Chambers.

An American student named John Wellborn Root was studying in Liverpool at the time and he later utilised many of the innovative features of the building in his own designs. The characteristic long rows of bay windows are evidenced in a number of skyscrapers that Root, together with his partner Daniel Hudson Burnham, designed in the 1880s. Both John Wellborn Root and Daniel Hudson Burnham were leading architects in the Chicago School of Architecture.

After sustaining some bomb damage during the Second World War, extensions were made to Oriel Chambers when it was repaired in 1950. The building was purchased in 2006 by Bruntwood.

## New Zealand House

Immediately after Oriel Chambers comes New Zealand House. Newz Bar was launched in New Zealand House by businessmen Paul and Julian Flanagan, transforming the former office equipment outlet into a trendy city centre brasserie bar. The Newz Bar was closed

New Zealand House.

in 2014, but after refurbishment businessman Riad Erraji opened the venue as the Amanzi restaurant. The restaurant flourished for some time, but it closed towards the end of 2015. Then, following a significant cash injection and another refurbishment, Know Restaurants Water Street Ltd transformed New Zealand House into a new restaurant known as District House; however, when the restaurant's parent company went into liquidation it was forced to close.

## West Africa House

West Africa House stands at the bottom of Water Street, on the southern corner that meets with the Strand. Designed by architects Briggs, Wolstenholme & Thornley, West Africa House was built in 1920. It was the same architectural team that designed the nearby Port of Liverpool Building. West Africa House was specially built for the Bank of British West Africa. The steel-framed building is faced with a discreet combination of Portland stone and Aberdeen granite, designed to reflect the importance of the owners.

When the bank closed the building remained empty for a number of years, before being opened as Grey Space Studios, a photographic studio specialising in photographing high-end fashion brands. The Bold Street tea shop Leaf acquired the lease in order to host private events and, more recently opened an exclusive venue in West Africa House called Oh Me Oh My – A Secret Space.

West Africa House.

## Tower Buildings

Tower Buildings stands on the corner of the Strand and Water Street, with its longer front on the eastern side of the Strand. The first building on the site is thought to have been built in or around 1256 and was believed to have been a sandstone mansion built near to the banks of the River Mersey. By 1360 the building was owned by Sir Robert Lathom, but by beginning of the ffifteenth century it was the property of Sir John Stanley. When Henry V granted Sir John permission to build a fortified house, the original house was demolished in 1406 and a much grander property known as the Tower of Liverpool was built. It was from this building – standing at the shore end of Water Street – that he administered his interests in the Isle of Man. The Corporation leased the Tower for a time, using part of the building as a prison. In 1774, the Corporation bought the building outright for £1535 10s and used it as the town's main prison for debtors and other criminals; however, on 3 July 1811 all of the inmates were transferred to the newly opened prison in Great Howard Street and it ceased to be a jail.

Towards the end of the eighteenth century the Tower fell into disrepair. In 1819, it was finally demolished so that Water Street could be widened. Following demolition, a number of warehouses were built on the site and remained as such until 1846 when Sir James Picton designed and built the second Tower Buildings. Sir James's design followed the Italianate style of architecture, but soon became the victim of changing commercial pressures and was replaced by the current building designed by Walter Aubrey Thomas and built between 1906 and 1910.

In 2006, the building was completely refurbished and converted into a number of apartments on the upper floors. The lower floors were reserved for commercial purposes until recently but are now being refurbished, ready for conversion into additional apartments. Tower Buildings is a Grade II-listed building.

*Above*: Tower Buildings, *c.* 1900.

*Below*: Tower Building.

## Cunard Building

After crossing the Strand, the building on the southern side of Water Street is the impressive Cunard Building, designed by William Edward Willink and Philip Coldwell Thicknesse. The building is one of Liverpool's Three Graces and is Grade II listed.

With the increase in transatlantic trade to and from Liverpool, the Cunard Line needed larger premises from which to co-ordinate their business as their current headquarters (also in Liverpool) was far too small for organisational efficacy. After considering a number of sites a suitable location was found between the Liver Building and the Port of Liverpool Building, both of which stood on the site of the former George's Dock. The building was constructed by Holland, Hannen & Cubitts between 1914 and 1917 in a style with both Italian Renaissance and Greek Revival influences. Similar to a number of other buildings in the vicinity, the architects chose to construct the building using reinforced concrete and clad it in Portland stone. The building is adorned with several sculptures including those of Britannia and Neptune, as well as a series that depicts different races from around the world, meant to reflect the global operational nature of the company.

When the Cunard White Star Line was formed in 1934 following the merger of the Cunard Steamship Co. and the White Star Line, the new company became the largest passenger steamship company in the world, effectively making Liverpool the most important centre of the British transatlantic industry. In addition to being the new company's headquarters, the Cunard Building also became the nerve centre for all the operational business of the company, having facilities for cruise liner passengers both prior to and after embarkation. There were also separate waiting rooms for first-, second- and third-class passengers, luggage storage space, the main booking hall and a dedicated currency exchange.

Looking up Water Street.

Cunard Building.

When the company's operational headquarters moved to Southampton in the 1960s, the building was sold to Prudential plc. Then, in November 2001, the building was sold to the Merseyside Pension Fund. Currently, the building provides office accommodation for a number of public and private sector organisations. At one time it was thought that the building might be used as a cruise liner terminal, with more liners now using the port, but the plans were thwarted due to the high costs associated with security and border control.

Because the Cunard Building was built after the Liver Building and Port of Liverpool Building, it meant that in order to maximise the space available the western sea-facing side needed to be built 30 feet narrower than the eastern landward side.

## Liver Building

The Liver Building, a Grade I-listed building, is perhaps Liverpool's most iconic building and stands opposite to the Cunard Buildings in Water Street. At 322 feet tall, the Liver Building has thirteen floors and is another of the Three Graces on the famous waterfront.

As far back as 1850 a group of nine men from Liverpool formed a burial society, with the sole aim of ensuring that their relatives would have sufficient funds to bury them when the time came. The society soon became known as the Liverpool Lyver Burial Society. By 1855, after phenomenal growth, they had opened a further twenty-five branches in other towns.

In 1856, the society took a different name: the Royal Liver Friendly Society. Their initial success prompted a move to a new headquarters in Prescot Street, but their continued success meant that a much larger headquarters was required.

3rd floor

Construction of the Liver Building, *c.* 1908.

Walter Aubrey Thomas was given the brief to design the new headquarters of the Royal Liver Group for 6,000 employees. The site chosen for the new office block was a plot of land that had previously been the site of George's Dock. The foundation stone for the new headquarters was laid on 11 May 1908 and just three years later, on 19 July 1911, the building was opened by Lord Sheffield.

A revolutionary building technique using reinforced concrete was adopted during the construction of the building, which many considered too complex to build because of its unique design. The Liver Building was the first major structure in the country and one of the first in the world to use this particular technique. The same revolutionary concept was later used in the construction of a number of skyscrapers in New York and Chicago.

The two liver birds that stand on the top of the building have a wingspan of 12 feet, stand 18 feet tall and are made of copper. The bird looking towards the sea is called Bella and the one that looks inland is called Bertie. Local legend has it that if the birds ever flew away then the city itself would die. The two birds – the symbol of Liverpool – were the work of German sculptor called Carl Bernard Bartels, a naturalised resident. During the First World War Bartels was arrested and imprisoned in an internment camp on the Isle of Man. At the end of the war he was forcibly repatriated to Germany.

The clocks on the two towers were made by Gent & Co. of Leicester. The clock faces are 25 feet in diameter. Before they were installed there was a unique dinner held for forty Royal Liver executives and civic dignitaries, with one of the clock faces being used as a dining table. The clocks are the largest electronic-driven clocks in the country and are controlled from the Greenwich Observatory. Originally called George clocks, they were started at 1.40 p.m. on 22 June 1911 – the precise time that George V was crowned.

The building was completely refurbished in the 1970s, with new heating and ventilating systems being introduced.

In February 2017, the Luxembourg-based investment group Corestate Capital bought the building for £48 million.

The Liver Building. *Inset*: The Liver Bird.

# 6. CHURCH STREET

Although Church Street isn't very long, it still rates as one of Liverpool's main shopping areas, but in many respects it was superseded with the creation of the Liverpool 1 retail area in October 2008. The street takes its name from the Church of St Peter, which was on the south side. The street runs into Lord Street to the west and to the east there is the once-fashionable Bold Street. The side streets to the north lead to Williamson Square and the streets to the south lead to the Grade I-listed Bluecoat Chambers. Our walk starts at the Lord Street end of Church Street.

The Church Street of today is very different from the Church Street of yesteryear. The cattle market that was once held here every week stopped a great many years ago. Until 1672 Church Street was a minor country lane. It was at this time that a bridge was built at the bottom of Lord Molyneux Street, crossing the original Pool. Sometime later, Mr Dansie, one of the town's leading merchants, built a fine mansion on the east side at the corner of

Church Street, 1940.

School Lane and Manesty Lane. At one time this property was used as Milners Safe Works, and it was here, in the cellar of the house, that the first Milners safes were manufactured.

Even in the middle of the eighteenth century there were no pavements along Church Street; it was much later – in 1816 – that the street was flagged. At that time there weren't that many shops, although there was a bookseller at the corner of Basnett Street. There was also a very famous confectioners shop at the corner of Church Alley. A post office was established in Church Street in 1800. The post office had previously been located in John Street, between Prince's Street and Dale Street.

A number of leading families in the town – including the Williamsons, the Tarletons and the Basnetts – laid out streets leading from Church Street. The Williamsons, like the Tarletons and the Basnetts, owned significant amounts of land and property in that area.

Williamson Street, which is the first street leading off to the north from Church Street, was laid out towards the end of the eighteenth century. Tarleton Street, the next street leading off from Church Street, is named after Banastre Tarleton (1754–1833) – perhaps the most infamous member of the family. His family were leading slave traders in Liverpool for at least three generations. The first Tarleton who was engaged in the notorious trade was Banastre's grandfather and following in his footsteps was Banastre's father. The third generation of Tarletons to be participants in the trade included Banastre himself and his brothers John, Clayton and Thomas.

During the American War of Independence General Banastre Tarleton won many plaudits for his valiance in the field of battle, which no doubt helped in his becoming elected as an MP for Liverpool in the general election of 1790. Following his election to Parliament, Tarleton continued to campaign for the continuation of the slave trade not only because of

Looking along today's Church Street.

Church Street.

the vested interest his family had in its continuation, but because of the undoubted wealth that it was continued to bring to Liverpool. In fact, during the whole of the time that the abolition of slave trading was being debated in Parliament and across the country, only one Liverpool MP publically voiced his opposition to its continuance: William Roscoe.

The final street leading off towards Williamson Square is Basnett Street. The first minister of the Key Street Presbyterian Chapel, near to Tithebarn Street, was Christopher Basnett.

## Compton Hotel

As ocean travel to and from America increased, so too did Liverpool's prosperity. In 1832, American brothers William and James Reddecliffe Jeffrey opened Compton House under the name of Jeffery & Co. The store sold a wide variety of products and, among other innovations, included a cabinetmaker, drapers and clothing department. It had five trading floors and many of the store's staff lived on the premises for convenience. The Grade II-listed building was built on the site where Marks & Spencer now stands and is believed to have been the first purpose-built department store anywhere in Europe, having been built some five years before Bon Marché in Paris.

On 8 December 1865, two police officers saw smoke coming from the basement of Compton House. A steam-powered fire engine was soon tackling the blaze, ably assisted by forty crew members from the HMS *Donegal* berthed nearby. Despite their efforts, by midnight that night only the blackened shell of the building remained. Over 1,000 jobs were lost. The building and contents were insured so rebuilding soon started and a new building was opened in 1867 on the same site. Unfortunately, the store never turned a profit and was forced to close in March 1871. It was later determined that the fire was started deliberately by one of Jeffery's employees.

The building was completely refurbished and opened as the Compton Hotel in 1873; William Russell was its first manager. The hotel, considered to be the best in town, catered mainly for American guests who arrived in Liverpool on the transatlantic steamers. The hotel boasted a number of high-quality shops on the ground floor, with 250 guest rooms on the floors above. The hotel's refinements included a billiard room, saloon, coffee room, reading room, writing room, smoking room, dining room, and even separate male and female drawing rooms. Because of the city's economic downturn in the 1920s, the hotel was forced to close its doors to guests in 1927. However, another transformation took place: Marks & Spencer, who had opened their first store in Liverpool's Lime Street in 1903, had the building refurbished and opened their flagship store in Liverpool in 1928. The store still occupies the same site.

## St Peter's Church

When the parish of Liverpool was established as being separate from the parish of Walton in 1699, two parish churches were built: St Peter's and Our Lady, and St Nicholas'. St Peter's was consecrated on 29 June 1704 and it was estimated that the building costs alone amounted to somewhat in excess of £4,000 – an astronomical

St Peter's Church, 1908.

figure at the time. St Peter's was widely considered to be the first parish church built in Lancashire following the Reformation, and up until the mid-eighteenth century it was the only building in the immediate vicinity. In 1830, a ring of ten bells was hung in the church.

When Liverpool gained city status in 1880 and was created a diocese in its own right, St Peter's was designated a pro-cathedral – a measure taken by Church authorities until a dedicated cathedral church could be built, as befitted a newly created city. There was, it must be said, the added incentive that with rising land prices the highly desirable location that St Peter's commanded ensured a good sale figure would be achieved.

A suitable site was found to build a cathedral upon and the church and surrounding area upon which St Peter's stood was sold in order to release equity for the building of the new cathedral. It was rumoured at one point that Harrods intended to buy the site and build their first store outside of London. In the event, the American company of F. W. Woolworth acquired the site, demolished the church and opened their first store in the United Kingdom. At the time it was demolished, St Peter's was thought to be the oldest building in the city.

The last service held at St Peter's was in September 1919 and although not standing today, the church is still remembered by a brass Maltese cross embedded in the pavement where L'Occitaine is now located.

*Below left*: St Peter's, Church Street.

*Below right*: An entrance to Liverpool 1 – the site of St Peter's.

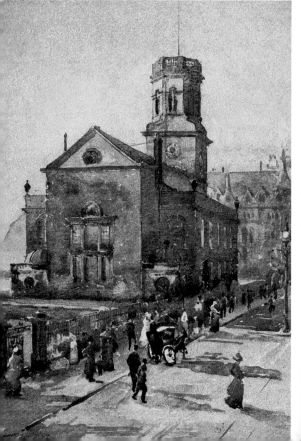

*Above*: The former Compton Hotel, now a branch of Marks & Spencer.

*Below left*: Looking along Church Alley towards the Bluecoat Chambers.

*Below right*: Looking towards Lord Street.

# 7. HOPE STREET

Hope Street is named in honour of William Hope, a local merchant whose house stood on the site now occupied by the Philharmonic Hall. The street itself stretches from Upper Parliament Street, past the Anglican Cathedral and as far as the Roman Catholic Cathedral. There are many notable buildings along the way, which collectively helped secure Hope Street the accolade of being the best street in the country and being awarded the Great Street award in the 2012 Urbanism Awards. The street was first straightened in the late eighteenth century and residential development started shortly after.

Before progressing further, a brief reflection on one of the more unpalatable events to occur in what many regard as one of Liverpool's most gentile streets. It was in 1826 that townsfolk in Liverpool were outraged when this particularly unsavoury crime was perpetrated. A cart coming from Hope Street carried three barrels of salted hides down to the docks for onward shipment to Glasgow. Once on board, a number of passengers noticed there was an unpleasant smell coming from the barrels. The decision was taken to offload them as passengers were objecting to their transportation. Unfortunately, one of the barrels burst open as it was being taken ashore; instead of containing salted hides there was a human body packed in salt. The other two barrels were also found to contain human bodies. Upon further investigation at the house in Hope Street, the police found thirty-three more

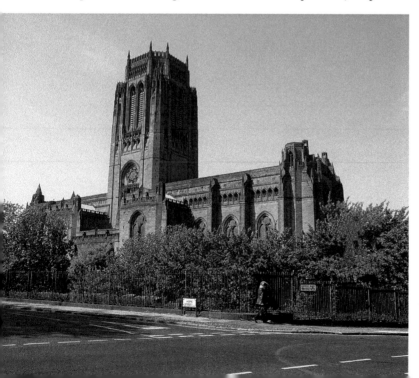

Liverpool Anglican Cathedral.

bodies. It transpired that all of them had been taken from the town's cemetery in Cambridge Street. During their investigations the police also discovered that there was a flourishing trade in cadavers, which were needed for medical students up and down the country.

## St James's Mount and Gardens

Starting at Upper Parliament Street and in the shadow of Liverpool's Anglican Cathedral, we walk along the entire length of St James's Mount and Gardens. The gardens were once a cemetery and before that a sandstone quarry (as early as the seventeenth century). By 1825 much of the stone had been excavated and the quarry was, in effect, exhausted. This posed a problem for the town council as something had to be done with the unsightly land. After raising almost £20,000 by public subscription, John Foster was employed and charged with designing a cemetery similar to Paris's famous cemetery of Père-la-Chaise. Soon after it was opened the cemetery became very busy, handling up to eight burials every day. After 57,774 burials it was considered to be full and it closed in July 1936. During the 1960s a plan was conceived to turn the cemetery into a public garden. Most of the many gravestones were removed so that an open landscape could be created. The gardens were completed and opened in 1972, whereas the Anglican Cathedral (more correctly referred to as the Cathedral Church of Christ in Liverpool) was not completed until later in the decade.

Following the installation of John Charles Ryle as the first bishop of Liverpool in 1880, it was decreed by an Act of Parliament in 1885 that a cathedral church should be built in Liverpool; however, the first designs and sites proved to be unsuitable. Following the induction of the second bishop, Francis Chavasse, other more suitable sites were identified for the building, the preferred option being St James's Mount. An open competition was then held, which was won by the twenty-two-year-old Giles Gilbert Scott. The foundation stone for the new cathedral was laid by Edward VIII in 1904.

Scott's original winning design had two towers at the west end and a single transept, but his revised design had a single central tower with twin transepts – radically different from the original design. Work went ahead, but it was severely curtailed during the First World War. Much progress was made on the building in the interwar years, but with the outbreak of the Second World War work was restricted yet again. The building was finally completed towards the latter part of the twentieth century. In October 1978, Elizabeth II attended a service of thanksgiving and dedication.

Along this section of Hope Street and running parallel on the right-hand side is Gambier Terrace, which shall be discussed later.

## Liverpool Institute of Performing Arts

We now come to the crossroads at the intersection of Upper Duke Street and Canning Street. After navigating the crossing you encounter a quaint Georgian building on the right masquerading as a newsagents – it's well worth a visit. The archetypal corner shop sells a wide range of snacks and confectionary as well as many magazines and the obligatory news print. Moving on, the Liverpool Institute of Performing Arts (LIPA) can now be seen to the left. LIPA occupies the site of what was formerly the Liverpool Institute for Boys – Paul McCartney's old school. Since 1998 John King's interesting sculpture, *A Case History*, has stood outside.

*A Case History.*

## Blackburne House

Walking along Hope Street there are many buildings worthy of note including Liverpool's Anglican Cathedral, Liverpool's Metropolitan Cathedral, the Liverpool Medical Institution, the Liverpool Masonic Hall, the Everyman Theatre, and Blackburne House – the next building that we come to on our right. The house was built in 1788 as a private dwelling for John Blackburne, a wealthy salt refiner who also had very heavy holdings in Liverpool's notorious slave trade. Blackburne House, like Blackburne Place where it stands, was named in his honour. He originally hailed from Orford, near Warrington, and was mayor of Liverpool in 1760.

Blackburne House is a Grade II-listed building. At the time of its construction the house was set in the countryside, outside of the town's boundaries.

In 1844, Blackburne sold the house to the cotton broker and abolitionist George Holt. A strong supporter of women's rights, Holt opened the property as Blackburne House Girls' School on 5 August 1844. The school was the first girls' school in Liverpool. Holt remained the school's director and president until his death in 1861. The school came under the jurisdiction of the city council in 1905; it closed in 1986. In 1994, the Women's Technology and Education Centre commissioned work at Blackburne House such that the premises could be converted into a training and resource centre.

Blackburne House.

## Ye Cracke

Next we come to Rice Street. Upon initial examination this street does not appear to have any buildings of outstanding merit or architectural value, but halfway along on the right is one of Liverpool's most celebrated pubs: a nineteenth-century pub called Ye Cracke. It's a quirky pub in many respects, but well worth a visit. Its main claim to fame is that John Lennon was a frequent visitor there when he was a student at the nearby art school.

Ye Cracke.

## Liverpool Hahnemann Hospital

Back in Hope Street, where any number of upmarket restaurants can be visited, we come to the Hahnemann Buildings. The year 1887 saw the opening of the Liverpool Hahnemann Hospital and Dispensary. The site was specifically chosen as it was the highest one available in the city and, according to the theory of the day, it was therefore the healthiest. It was the sugar merchant and philanthropist Henry Tate who had the facility built and equipped at his own expense. The gesture was intended as a gift to the citizens of Liverpool and provided treatment for the poor of the city. Local architect F. & G. Holme designed the building, which had fifty-two beds and operated as a public general hospital. The design and fitting out of the hospital, especially with regards to the ward layout, ventilation and heating, closely followed principles and practices as advocated by Florence Nightingale. Ward hygiene was also a key consideration and for this reason many of the inside walls of the building were clad with glazed tiles. The need for good hygiene was imperative and extended throughout the whole of the hospital regime. It was this philosophy that prompted the building of an addition to the south west of the hospital in 1903, providing nurses accommodation, a washhouse and a laundry.

During First World War, the War Office requisitioned the hospital to be used as an auxiliary military hospital. Then, during the Second World War the hospital became part of the Emergency Medical Services. In 1948, the hospital came under state control following the National Health Service Act of 1946 and became part of the South Liverpool Group of Hospitals, taking the name of the Liverpool Homeopathic Hospital. The name was changed again in 1969 to the Hahnemann Hospital and then in 1972 it became part of the United Liverpool Hospitals. The hospital closed in 1976. In recent years the building has

John Moores University Buildings.

formed part of Liverpool John Moores University, with the former wards being used by the Liverpool School of Art and Design.

The Hahnemann Buildings, as they are now called, are a designated Grade II-listed building and currently being used as student accommodation.

## Philharmonic Hall

Next we come to the Philharmonic Hall on the right, home of the Royal Liverpool Philharmonic Orchestra, which celebrated its 175th anniversary in 2015. Before the first Philharmonic Hall was built a mill stood on the site. At one time there was also an observatory in the immediate area, which was erected to assist the comings and goings of the increasingly busy port; however, shortly after completion the observatory fell into disrepair.

The Philharmonic Society was established in 1842 and meetings were held in Great Richmond Street. After much initial success, it was considered that a more suitable building must be established. The funds necessary to erect the new building were raised in shares and in return subscribers were promised boxes and stalls in the new building.

The original Philharmonic Hall.

The Philharmonic Hall.

The original Liverpool Philharmonic Hall was opened on 27 August 1849 and was reputedly 'the best in Europe'. Unfortunately, the hall was completely destroyed in 1933 due to a fire.

Since the new hall was opened in 1939 there have been two major refurbishments: the first, in 1995, cost £10.3 million and restored much of the art deco splendour of the hall; the second, in 2013, made changes to the front-of-house areas, built new rehearsal and backstage facilities, carried out improvements to the box office and bar areas, and gave lift access to all levels.

## Philharmonic Dining Rooms

At the corner of Hope Street and Hardman Street, opposite the Philharmonic Hall, is the Philharmonic Dining Rooms, a public house more usually referred to as 'The Phil'. The Phil is a Grade II-listed building.

A local brewer named Robert Cain built the public house between 1898 and 1900. Walter W. Thomas designed the building in conjunction with staff from the School of Architecture and Applied Arts at University College, which later became part of the University of Liverpool.

If you happen to pay a visit to The Phil, be sure to call in at the gent's while you're there. This may sound like a bizarre request, but the gent's urinals are constructed in a very delicate roseate marble and famous throughout the North West.

Philharmonic Dining Rooms.

## Liverpool Masonic Hall

On the same side as the Philharmonic Dining Rooms at No. 22 Hope Street is the Liverpool Masonic Hall. Before moving their meeting place to Hope Street, a committee of leading Masons was formed with the specific brief to purchase a property that would be a suitable venue for Liverpool lodges to meet. A house in Hope Street, 'The House in the Garden', was purchased. On April 23 1858 the committee met to discuss the possibility of converting the property for the purposes of Freemasonry. After making some necessary alterations to the property, the Masonic Hall was opened on 8 October 1858. But by 1872 the property was deemed not to be suitable for purpose and demolished.

The corner stone of a new specially built Masonic Hall was laid on 2 November and the hall itself opened in 1874. Later, because of the increasing popularity of Freemasonry, extensions had to be considered. Fortunately, a strip of land to the side of the existing hall became available for purchase, but it was not until after the vicissitudes of the First World War had ceased that the building work was finally completed in 1932.

## Everyman Theatre

On the far side of the road is the newly rebuilt Everyman Theatre. The history of the Everyman itself goes back to 1964, but the original building on the site – from 1837 – was a Nonconformist chapel. Hope Hall, as it was called, became a church dedicated to Saint John the Evangelist in 1841. Further changes were on the way, and in 1853 the church became the Public Hall and Concert Hall. Later, in 1912, the hall was once again reincarnated, becoming Hope Hall Cinema. The hall continued in this guise until it finally closed in 1963. But, before the hall finally closed, it had become the preferred meeting place of a group of poets and local artists collectively known as the Liverpool Scene. They conceived the idea of turning the venue into a theatre of performing arts. The Everyman Theatre opened in September 1964. Being located in an area noted for its bohemian environment and political awareness, it is not surprising that the Everyman soon gained a reputation for staging groundbreaking productions.

In 1975 the theatre closed for rebuilding, and while the work was carried out a touring company was formed. The newly refurbished theatre was opened in 1977. Many local writers and artists were showcased during the 1970s and 1980s including writers

Everyman Theatre.

Willy Russell and Alan Bleasdale, and actors Julie Walters, Pete Postlethwaite, Jonathan Pryce, Bernard Hill, Matthew Kelly and Bill Nighy.

The Liverpool and Merseyside Theatres Trust has managed both the Everyman and the Liverpool Playhouse since 2004. The theatres operate an integrated programme that is jointly managed by their artistic director and executive director.

The Everyman closed in July 2011 in order to be completely rebuilt and refurbished. Architects Haworth Tompkins designed the new theatre. The cost of rebuilding was £27 million, with much of the funding coming from Arts Council England and the European Regional Development Fund. When the theatre reopened in February 2014 it was recognised as being the best British building of the year and awarded the Stirling Prize by the Royal Institute of British Architects.

## Liverpool's Metropolitan Cathedral

Last along this historic street, we arrive at Liverpool's Metropolitan Cathedral, although strictly speaking the cathedral's address is Mount Pleasant. The cathedral is more properly known as the Metropolitan Cathedral of Christ the King,

Due largely to the influx of Irish Roman Catholics into Liverpool in the nineteenth century –fleeing from the Great Irish Famine (1845–52) – it was considered that there needed to be a Catholic cathedral in the city.

Liverpool Roman Catholic Cathedral.

Roman Catholic Cathedral during construction, *c.* 1965.

   Edward Welby Pugin was awarded the commission to build the new cathedral and by
1856 the Lady chapel had been completed; however, due to the financial resources having
to be used for the education of Catholic children, work on the cathedral ceased.

   The former workhouse site on Brownlow Hill was purchased in 1930 and Sir Edwin
Lutyens was commissioned to design a cathedral befitting a flourishing city. The design was
truly momentous and would have become the second-largest church in the world. Work
started on Whit Monday, 5 June 1933, but, similar to the fate that befell the city's Anglican
Cathedral, work had to stop during the Second World War. Work resumed in 1956 and the
cathedral's crypt was completed in 1958. Due to spiralling costs it was considered that the
expenditure could not be justified and no further work on Lutyens design was sanctioned.

   A competition to design the cathedral was held in 1959. It was stated among the design
requirements that the cathedral must be able to accommodate a congregation of 3,000 –
later modified to 2,000. A second requirement was that all of the congregation should
be able to clearly see the altar during services. The competition was won by Frederick
Gibberd, who submitted a cathedral design that was circular in concept and was to be
constructed in concrete with Portland stone cladding. Construction began in 1962 and the
cathedral was consecrated on 14 May 1967 – the feast of Pentecost.

# 8. GAMBIER TERRACE

Gambier Terrace is named in honour of Admiral James Gambier, who first distinguished himself on the 'Glorious First of June' in 1794. In 1807, he was commander of the British fleet at Copenhagen. To honour this victory he was awarded a peerage. From 1808 to 1811 he was in command of the Channel fleet. He was subsequently appointed as governor of Newfoundland in Canada.

The building of the terrace was primarily brought about due to the rate at which Liverpool was expanding during the early nineteenth century. As a direct result of this expansion, many of the town's more affluent residents were demanding higher-quality housing away from the town centre. Gambier Terrace was planned sometime between 1830 and 1835. It is thought that the terrace was designed by John Foster Jr. When originally conceived it was to be built in a single style, but building work came to an abrupt halt during the slump of 1837 and when the market picked up again many years later styles and tastes had changed. Subsequent properties along the terrace were built to a lower specification, as the railways were now taking people to more outlying and desirable destinations. No. 10 Gambier Terrace was the last property to be built to Foster's original design and Nos 1–10 are Grade II-listed buildings.

Standing in Gambier Terrace and looking over towards the Anglican Cathedral, St James's Cemetery and Mount Gardens are directly ahead. The cemetery – now classed as an urban park – stands below ground level and has been designated as a Grade I Historic Park. The original park was established in 1771 and is thought to have been the first public park in Liverpool. The area was originally known as Quarry Hill and during the early eighteenth century the quarry – from where the area took its name – was the source

Gambier Terrace.

of building materials for many of the town's public buildings including the Town Hall, St John's, St Thomas's and St Paul's churches. The elevation was an ideal location for the windmill that stood on Quarry Hill.

Foster built a windowless oratory on higher ground towards the northern end. The original purpose of this Grecian-style building was to act as a mortuary. Funeral services were also held there before the actual burial ceremony.

Documentary evidence shows that the freehold to Gambier Terrace and the gardens to the front is held by Liverpool City Council, but the exact legal status of the land is still open to interpretation. The area is jointly maintained by the council and the leaseholders, although the public thoroughfare remains unadopted by the council.

Within days of the outbreak of the First World War, a young doctor named Mary Birrell Davies determined that additional resources would be needed in order to maintain the morale of the troops at the Front and the communities at home who supported them. On 7 August 1914 she formed the Women's War Service Bureau. The Bureau originally distributed food parcels from its headquarters at No. 1 Gambier Terrace to troops serving in local regiments at the Front. As the service became more established and demand grew, other services were provided such as the collection and distribution of garments, sending bandages and other medical supplies to field hospitals. Volunteers working for the Bureau also made and altered clothes for soldiers. With the work growing at such an alarming rate, the premises at No. 1 Gambier Terrace soon became insufficient for the range of services that the Bureau was now providing, so additional premises were secured throughout the city centre.

By the end of the First World War the Bureau's *raison d'être* was redundant, but upon commencement of the Second World War the Women's War Service Bureau was again set up, this time at Nos 9, 11 and 12 Gambier Terrace.

In 1960, Stuart Sutcliffe, the so-called 'Fifth Beatle' lived at No. 3 Gambier Terrace while he was a student at the Liverpool College of Art. Having a degree of compassion for a fellow student who was homeless at the time, Sutcliffe appealed to the other residents to allow his friend to stay at the property, to which they agreed; the friend was John Lennon!

*Below left*: View of the Anglican Cathedral from Gambier Terrace.

*Below right*: The Oratory in St James's Gardens.

*Above*: Looking towards Gambier Terrace from St James's Gardens.

*Below left*: Huskisson Monument in St James's Gardens.

*Below right*: No. 3 Gambier Terrace, sometime home of John Lennon.

# 9. RODNEY STREET

After buying much of the land in the area, it was William Roscoe who laid out Rodney Street between 1783 and 1784. Roscoe was born in Liverpool on 8 March 1753, the son of a market gardener who also kept a public house in the town centre.

The initial route of Rodney Street was projected in the late eighteenth century and extended from Mount Pleasant to Upper Duke Street. Many still consider that the new street was originally to be called Schlink Street, in order to commemorate the name of a Dutchman who had bought a sizable amount of land in the immediate area. However, so the story goes, when it became known that the land was to be used to rear calves for veal, the name was changed – in 1782 – to Rodney Street in honour of George Brydges Rodney, 1st Baron Rodney. During a three-day battle against the French off the Dominican coast in April 1782 – the Battle of the Saintes – Brydges commanded the British fleet, capturing seven French battleships together with the French commanding officer, Count François de Grasse. For his services to the country, Brydges was made 1st Baron Rodney. He was also awarded a pension of some £2,000 per annum. At the time English morale was very low, after having suffered the humiliating defeat in America but this victory ensured that Britain maintained influence in the West Indies.

At the time of its construction there was also another street in the town called Rodney Street, but the name was changed to Admiral Street in order to avoid any confusion. Many merchants in Liverpool at this time were still in receipt of profits accruing from the slave trade. In fact, Rodney himself, like so many of his contemporaries, was a firm advocate of it, speaking against abolition in the House of Lords. Roscoe, on the other hand, was vehemently against it and argued strongly in favour of abolition when he was elected to Parliament.

At the beginning of the nineteenth century much of the land in and around Hope Street, Upper Duke Street and Rodney Street was not built upon, but remained either open land or cultivated fields. The area was covered in heather and there were many sandpits in the immediate vicinity. There was a quarry to the east side of this area, and to the north, beyond the junction of Rodney Street and Upper Parliament Street, stood one of Liverpool's many windmills. There was also a tavern and a bowling green nearby.

When building did start, the street was developed in a somewhat haphazard manner, with large houses of varying dimensions being built for many of the town's more affluent citizens. At the time, Rodney Street lay outside of the town's boundaries, and properties were in great demand from wealthy tradespeople and merchants seeking a more tranquil environment some distance from the day-to-day hustle and bustle of the fast-developing sea port. Generally speaking, the houses were built in pairs or in small blocks, hence the different roof lines along the street.

Compared to many of Liverpool's other illustrious streets, Rodney Street may be somewhat lacking in its kerb appeal, but first appearances can be deceptive. Even so, the building of Rodney Street was a somewhat protracted affair, continuing for a period of almost forty years. By 1825 most of the building work was complete.

Though early residents in Rodney Street were drawn from many different professions, including local government officials, serving army officers and bankers, many of the residents were from the medical profession, including the pioneer Ambrose Dawson MD. This is still the case today, with many surgeons and specialists retaining consulting rooms in the street. Rodney Street is often referred to as the 'Harley Street of the North'.

## No. 4 Rodney Street

Rodney Street runs from Mount Pleasant right through to Upper Duke Street, crossing the junction with Leece Street and Hardman Street on its way. Beginning at the Mount Pleasant end of the street, the first house of any note is No. 4, where the first consul from the United States – James Maury – lived from 1790 to 1829. No. 4 was also where Brian Epstein, manager of the Beatles, was born in 1934.

## Scottish Presbyterian Church of Saint Andrew

Just across the road we see the imposing structure of the Scottish Presbyterian Church of Saint Andrew. The body of the church was designed by Daniel Stewart and the façade is the work of John Foster Jr, the senior surveyor of the Corporation of Liverpool. The church opened on 3 December 1824 with Dr David Thorn as its first minister. The church and graveyard was initially leased by the Corporation of Liverpool for a period of seventy-five years. In 1825 disagreements surfaced between Dr Thorn and some members of his congregation so a commission was established to consider all of the allegations. As a result of the findings,

Scottish
Presbyterian
Church of
St Andrew.

Dr Thorn ceased to be the church's minister. Some members of the congregation followed him to another chapel, where he continued to minister until shortly before his death.

After many years of neglect the church fell into disrepair. Eventually, in 2008, it was purchased by Liverpool City Council and a sum of £150,000 was needed for emergency repairs. The building was subsequently acquired by Liverpool John Moores University, refurbished and opened as St Andrew's Place, providing accommodation for 100 students. During the refurbishment part of the exterior was remodelled.

The pyramidal William Mackenzie monument has stood in the churchyard since 1868. The monument is a Grade II-listed structure and was erected in memory of William Mackenzie (d. 1851), a railway contractor who was also known to be a gambling man. Urban mythology maintains that because of financial problems caused through gambling, he was forced to sell his soul to the Devil. But, with characteristic guile, Mackenzie had his tomb built in such a way that he now sits – within the pyramid-like structure – above the ground so that the Devil cannot claim his soul. As a result, it is also rumoured that his ghost haunts Rodney Street.

## Famous Residents

### Arthur Hugh Clough

The poet Arthur Hugh Clough was born at No. 9 Rodney Street on 1 January 1819. In 1822, the family moved to the United States, but just a few years later – 1828 – Clough and his elder brother Charles returned to Liverpool to complete their education. In later life, Clough spent considerable time campaigning for hospital reform with his wife's cousin, Florence Nightingale.

### Henry Booth

A little further along at No. 34 Rodney Street is the house where Henry Booth was born. He was destined to follow in his father's footsteps and become a corn merchant, but his true vocation was as a railway engineer. He became a founder and director of the Liverpool & Manchester Railway.

Henry Booth's birthplace.

### Edward Fitzmaurice Chambré Hardman

Moving along, we come to No. 59, one-time home and studio of the photographer Edward Fitzmaurice Chambré Hardman. Although a native of Dublin, Edward Fitzmaurice Chambré Hardman spent most of his working life as a photographer in Liverpool. It was when Hardman was serving in the army that he met Captain Kenneth Burrell, who also had a keen interest in photography. Upon leaving the army they went into business together in Liverpool. The successful partnership lasted for many years.

In 1932, Hardman married his assistant, Margaret Mills. They worked together and their portrait business thrived during the Second World War. After the war they moved into larger premises at No. 59 Rodney Street, which was to remain their home and studio for the rest of their lives. Margaret died in 1970 and Hardman lost not only a constant companion but a skilled photographer, tireless worker and able business partner. Subsequently, Hardman's health also suffered, although he did continue with some exhibition work. Hardman died on 2 April 1988. His home and studio in Rodney Street are now conserved by the National Trust.

### William Gladstone

No. 62 is perhaps one of the most significant properties along Rodney Street as this is where the wealthy Scottish slave-owning merchant Sir John Gladstone lived with his second wife, Anne MacKenzie Robertson. Their fourth son, William Ewart Gladstone, was born there on 29 December 1809. Gladstone's residency in Rodney Street was relatively short-lived, however, as the family moved to Seaforth House in 1816.

*Below left*: Edward Hardman's studio.

*Below right*: One of the many grand façades along Rodney Street.

Gladstone's birthplace.

William Gladstone served as prime minister on four separate occasions. He also held the high office of Chancellor of the Exchequer on four separate occasions.

Much later, in 1932, when the house had been divided into two properties, the Earl of Derby opened No. 62 as a Toc H hostel.

### Nicholas Monsarrat

Other famous people who have lived in Rodney Street include Nicholas Monsarrat, who was born there on 22 March 1910. Although trained as a lawyer, Monsarrat soon turned to writing.

During the Second World War Lieutenant Commander Nicholas John Turney Monsarrat FRSL RNVR was a member of the Royal Naval Volunteer Reserve (RNVR). Following his distinguished war career, Monsarrat entered the diplomatic service and served in South Africa and Canada. He became a full-time writer in 1959. Arguably, his most famous novels are: *The Cruel Sea* (1951), *Three Corvettes* (1945), *The Tribe That Lost Its Head* (1956) and its sequel *Richer Than All His Tribe* (1968).

Monsarrat died of cancer on 8 August 1979 and, following his wishes, was buried at sea.

### Max Arbis

Over the years, as the houses became too big for single occupancy, other trades and professions utilised the potential offered by the grand scale of the properties. A number of privately funded educational establishments were located in the prestigious street, as were some small hotels. For many years, No. 16 Rodney Street was also the business premises of one of the city's most famous tailors, Max Arbis.

Note

In the vicinity of Rodney Street, Gambier Terrace and Hope Street (collectively known as the Rodney Street Conservation Area) there are in excess of sixty Grade II-listed buildings.

Our walk ends at the junction with Upper Duke Street with the inspiring sight of Liverpool's Anglican Cathedral directly in front of us.

Upper Duke Street end of Rodney Street.

# 10. ABERCROMBY SQUARE

Sir Ralph Abercromby (1734–1801) was general commander of the British Army in Egypt. He was killed at the Battle of Alexandra in 1801. Abercromby Square was named in his honour. There is also a memorial to him in St Paul's Cathedral, London.

Towards the latter part of the eighteenth century, the areas around Mount Pleasant and Brownlow Hill were being developed as many of Liverpool's more affluent residents desired houses with gardens. They also wanted to be closer to fields and open spaces.

Recognising the financial benefits of building properties in this area, the town's Corporation took the decision to build their own development in Moss Lake Fields in close proximity to both Brownlow Hill and Mount Pleasant. The Corporation's senior surveyor, John Foster, drew up the plans and they were agreed in 1801. The central feature of the development was to be a magnificent square: Abercromby Square.

A considerable amount of effort was expended in preparing the land for building. As the site was often water-logged, suitable drainage had to be laid so that water could be drained via a tunnel. In fact, Moss Lake itself, together with the surrounding areas of Crown Street and Grove Street, were often under water. In winter when the whole area was frozen over, the lake became a favourite spot for skaters.

The area upon which the exclusive properties were to be built was fenced off with railings that were in keeping with the type of properties being built. It was anticipated

War memorial.

that these railings would prevent any cattle and other animals straying onto the land. The houses were primarily targeted at the more affluent residents of the town, having imposing residential styles of classical architecture. The council did not develop the land themselves, but awarded contract for the development and the subsequent lease to a merchant in Liverpool, Mr Lawson, and to another of Liverpool's leading residents, Mr Pritt. The council laid down some very strict conditions in the contract; for instance, the footwalks in the front of the houses were to be paved with strong flags and the surrounding streets were to be paved with small pebbles. Other conditions stated that the properties were not to be used for the carrying out of any offensive trades and that the cellars must not be used for any merchandising or for subletting for separate habitation.

## Abercromby Square Gardens

Similarly, no effort was spared when it came to the design of what was to become known as Abercromby Square Gardens, or, as it was known locally, the Shrubbery. The curator of Liverpool's Botanic Garden, John Shepherd, was consulted. In addition to the planting, a domed garden house was erected in the centre of the gardens. The gardens retained their exclusivity as cast-iron railings were placed around the perimeter, and for an annual subscription of 1 guinea those residing in houses surroundings the gardens were issued with a key to access them.

Abercromby Square Gardens.

Prominent Residents

A number of the town's prominent residents chose to move to Abercromby Square, including the Mozleys, Langtons, Ripleys and the Doerings, following the lead of established residents such as the Littledales, Gladstones and Earles. There was a degree of incongruity in the development, however, as although it was fast becoming the residential area of choice for the affluent and famous, it was also home to Liverpool's women's prison, an asylum, one of the town's infamous workhouses, numerous almshouses, and the adjacent area of Myrtle Street was also famed for its many brothels.

As the town developed and spread out Abercromby Square lost much of its exclusivity, with many of the more affluent residents choosing to move to other areas. However, a number of senior professionals from the town moved into the area including the borough engineer, James Newlands. A number of the town's surgeons also chose Abercromby Square as their place of residence.

No. 19 Abercromby Square was the last house to be built on the north side of the square. The house was designed for the banker Mr Charles Kuhn Prioleau, a native American and supporter of the confederate south. He settled in Liverpool in 1854 and became a naturalised citizen in 1863. The property was later to become the Bishop's Palace when Liverpool became a diocese in its own right. Bishop John Charles Ryle was created as Liverpool's first Anglican bishop on 19 April 1880. The second bishop of Liverpool, who also lived at No. 19 Abercromby Square, was Bishop Francis James Chavasse. He

*Below left*: Blue plaque for Noel Chavasse.

*Below right*: Former Bishop's Palace.

was enthroned on 31 May 1900. One of Bishop Chavasse's seven children, his son Noel served as a surgeon during the First World War attached to the 10th Battalion of the King's Liverpool Regiment, the Liverpool Scottish. He was the only man ever to be awarded two Victoria Crosses – the second being posthumously awarded.

## University of Liverpool

In the twentieth century, the whole of the north side of Abercromby Square was acquired by the University of Liverpool due to the foresight of Charles Reilly (professor of architecture, who advocated the development of Abercromby Square for the university) and the benevolence of Charles Sydney Jones, who was a wealthy shipowner and treasurer of the university.

Most of the buildings in and around Abercromby Square are now owned by the University of Liverpool. The university's Department of Education occupies the former Bishop's Palace.

Looking across Abercromby Square to the university's Department of Education.

# SELECT BIBLIOGRAPHY

Baines, Thomas, *History of the Commerce and Town of Liverpool in 1859* (British Library, Historical Print Editions).

Baines, Thomas, *Liverpool in 1859* (Benson & Mallett).

Baines, Thomas, *The Port and Town of Liverpool in 1860.*

Brooke, Richard, *Liverpool As It Was: 1775–1800* (Liverpool Libraries and Information Service).

Brown, Alexander, *Smith's Strangers' Guide to Liverpool, its Environs, and Part of Cheshire, for 1843.*

Enfield, William, *An Essay Towards the History of Liverpool* (1774).

Horton, Steven, *Street Names of the City of Liverpool* (Countyvise Limited: 2002).

*A New Illustrated Guide to Liverpool* (Cromwell Press Ltd: 2004).

Muir, Ramsay, *A History of Liverpool* (Williams & Norgate: 1907).

Muir, Ramsay, *Bygone Liverpool 1913* (Henry Young & Sons).

*Liverpool Through the Lens: Photography of Edward Chambre Hardman* (National Trust Books: 2007).

Paul, David, *Thetis: Submarine Disaster* (Fonthill Media: 2014).

Paul, David, *Central Liverpool* (Tempus Publishing: 1997).

Phillips, R., 'Castle Street' in Wallace, James, *A General and Descriptive History of the Ancient and Present State of the Town of Liverpool.*

Pickton, James, *Memorials of Liverpool, Including A History of the Dock Estate: Vol. 1* (Longmans, Green & Co.: 1873).

Postance, R., *Old Liverpool: Written In Manuscript* (1889).

Reilly, C. H., *Some Liverpool Streets and Buildings in 1921* (*Liverpool Daily Post & Mercury*: 1921).

Stonehouse, James, *The Streets of Liverpool* (Liverpool Libraries and Information Services: 2002).

Wilkinson, Colin, *The Streets of Liverpool: Volume 2* (The Bluecoat Press: 2012).

# ACKNOWLEDGEMENTS

It would be nigh-on impossible to thank all the people who have helped me in the writing of this book, but I must make special mention of the staff at the Central Library in Liverpool, whose ever-ready help and knowledge has both assisted and encouraged me in this endeavour. I also wish to thank Frank Lyons for his diligence in locating some of the more obscure manuscripts, which have verified a number of historical facts.

Also, with reference to some of the photographs included in the book, I wish to state that despite prolonged and exhaustive enquiries, tracking down some copyright holders has not been possible.

Finally, while I have tried to ensure that the information is factually correct – a daunting task in itself – any errors or inaccuracies are mine alone.

# ABOUT THE AUTHOR

David Paul was born and brought up in Liverpool. Following a number of years working for the Liverpool-based Pacific Steam Navigation Co., David returned to his native city to teach Marine Engineering at Riversdale Technical College.

Since retiring, David has written a number of books on different aspects of Liverpool's history.

## Also by David Paul

*Eyam: Plague Village*
*Speke to Me*
*Around Speke Through Time*
*Woolton Through Time*
*Anfield Voices*
*Illustrated Tales of Lancashire*